Trade Like a Monk

Trade Like a Monk

Master Your Mind, Master the Markets

HARNEET SINGH KHARBANDA

JAICO PUBLISHING HOUSE

Ahmedabad Bangalore Chennai
Delhi Hyderabad Kolkata Mumbai

Published by Jaico Publishing House
A-2 Jash Chambers, 7-A Sir Phirozshah Mehta Road
Fort, Mumbai - 400 001
jaicopub@jaicobooks.com
www.jaicobooks.com

TRADE LIKE A MONK
ISBN 978-93-49358-70-6

First Jaico Impression: 2026
Second Jaico Impression: 2026

Page design and layout by R. Ajith Kumar, Delhi

Printed by
Repro India Limited, Mumbai

This book is dedicated to my parents,
my wife and both my lovely daughters.

DISCLAIMER

This book should be treated only as educational material. The technical charts or stocks mentioned should not be treated as investment or trading advice. This book has been written to make the readers aware of the importance of trading psychology in the field of trading and investing. Please consult your financial advisor before entering the stock market or investing your hard-earned money.

CONTENTS

PART 2: INTERVIEWS

PREFACE

While interacting with a trader or investor—whether they are seasoned players of the markets or just starting their journey in the exciting realm of stock markets—one thing I found in common was that everyone focused too much on the technical and strategy aspects of trading. Almost everyone ignored the psychological aspects. I have been trading full-time in the stock markets for the last 10 years, and I am quite active on social media as well. I have interacted with thousands of traders and investors via social media platforms, and directly while attending offline trading and investing conferences across India.

If you interact with a professional trader or investor, they would tell you how much trading psychology helped them become better traders or investors. In fact, trading psychology and mindset make up 80% of being a better trader or investor. If everyone could become a better trader just by being good at technical or fundamental analysis, all the chartered market technicians (CMTs) and chartered financial analysts (CFAs) of the world would have been the ones dominating the markets. However, we have seen that the great investors and traders have humble educational backgrounds, but have mastered their trading and investing by conquering their mind.

It is "You vs. You" here, rather than "You vs. the Markets".

ACKNOWLEDGMENTS

I am grateful to all the mentors who have helped me, directly or indirectly, become a better trader.

I will always be grateful to one person, without whom even this book would not have been possible—Indrazith Shantharaj. I met him in Bengaluru a few years ago. Even though he did not know me personally and we had just interacted a few times over Twitter messages till then, he took the time to meet me and over two days explained each and every thing about writing a book. Indrazith helped me day in and day out to prepare this book.

When he had published his first book a few years ago, he faced many problems. So he wanted to make sure that I don't go through all those hardships. He literally paved the way so well that I could write this book with ease.

I want to thank all the amazing traders whom I have interviewed for this book. Many traders try to hide their trading style and like to keep it to themselves. So I was worried whether I would be able to convince them to be a part of this book. To my surprise, all the traders I asked, agreed right away!

1 MASTER YOUR MIND

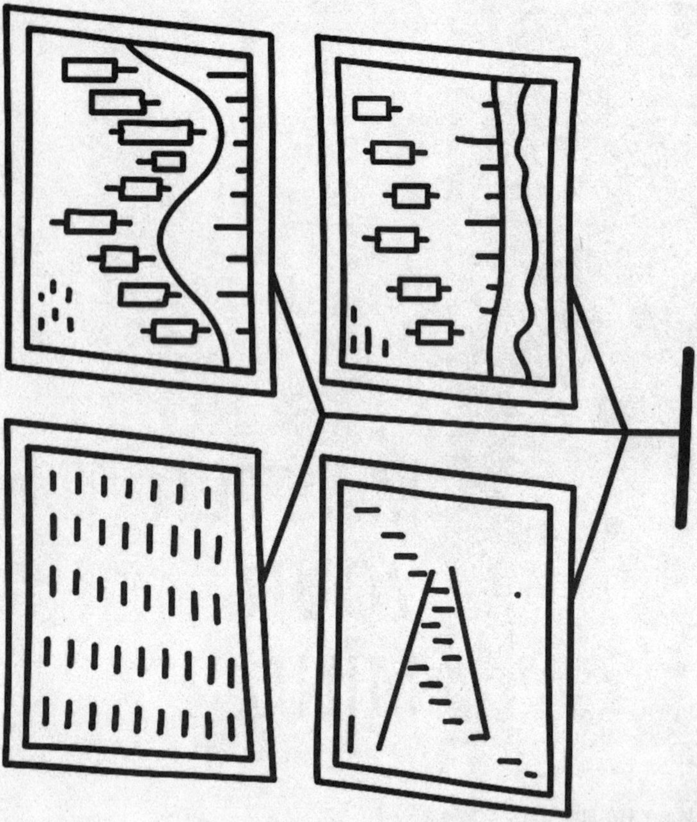

01

THE FLICKERING LIGHTS

THE MILLIONS THAT I LOST IN THE STOCK MARKET, TAUGHT ME LESSONS WORTH BILLIONS!

Are you a new trader and want to make it big in the stock market?

Are you fascinated by the red and green flickering numbers on the screen and want to know how they work?

Have you heard amazing stories of some legendary investors or traders who have made it big in the stock market, and now want to walk on the same path?

Have you always wanted to understand what the technical charts indicate and how you can use them to make *real* money?

These are some of the questions that every new trader has in his mind. They just want to enter the realm of the stock market—full of excitement—and make it to the top. While passion and excitement are the fuel to fulfill any desire, plan carefully and do groundwork, before jumping into the ocean of the stock market.

The most common mistake that people make is that they enter the market half-prepared or, let us face it, not prepared at all. Fascinated by the huge success stories of some legendary traders and investors, they start seeing themselves in their shoes. However, in any other occupation or profession, we need to complete a few years of formal studies followed by higher studies and finally an internship or practice sessions before landing a job that makes us money.

In the case of the stock market, you can just open a Demat account and start trading immediately. The irony is, you have a chance of being right 50% of the time! Stocks can either move up or down, so you have a chance of being right on your very first trade—believe me, there is something called "beginner's luck," and it is often seen that your first trade generally goes in your favour.

It might sound good. But it is actually the worst thing that can happen to a new trader as it gives them the illusion that it is effortless to make money in the stock market. The profit that the trader made in their first attempt will induce them to multiply it with the days of the week, month, and even the entire year and get a false idea of how much they can *actually* make. It is one of the most crucial factors creating a false baseline for what is to come. Once people get a taste of quick money, they get hooked. After that, there is no looking back, and they often keep trading without any plan until it is too late.

There is no doubt that only 10% of traders can make it big, because it takes a lot of dedication and experience to trade successfully, and knowledge is the first step of all the variables. Your decision to buy and read this book is a sign that you are passionate about the markets and ready to put in the work. That is why you have decided to gain more knowledge about trading rather than just diving into it like everyone else. So I want to congratulate and welcome you to the fascinating world of stock markets.

Let me tell you a story. There was a young boy, very enthusiastic about markets. Let us call him Rahul. Rahul's family was involved in the cloth business. Once he completed his studies, he would work there. After being a part of this business for a few years, he realised that although he was making good money, his heart was not really in it. He also understood that making money and how you do it are two different things. Although his family business was reaching new peaks, he felt empty and hollow inside. He wanted to pursue an occupation he really enjoyed, something he would even love to do for free!

Rahul had heard about the stock market from his friends when he was in college but did not take it seriously. There had been many devastating accounts of his father's friends and relatives who had lost an enormous amount in the markets. He did not think about the stock market after that till he met someone who was making a living from full-time trading. He got very excited and wanted to learn more about it. The trader explained, as many people make losses, it is evident that a few take away all the money in the form of profits. So there has to be an equilibrium in the markets in the short term. He requested the trader to teach him everything about the markets. The trader accepted his request and invited him to his house the following day. Once there, Rahul noticed that even though the trader had a multi-screen setup, he was not glued to the screens and just glanced at the rates once in a while. He looked at ease and was not worried by the red and green lights constantly flickering in front of him. For Rahul, the office and setup were love at first sight. He knew in a heartbeat that this was what he wanted to do for the rest of his life. He already made money in his family business, but he did not like the way he was making it. He had to literally beg customers who took goods on credit to pay up. He was frustrated with the unprofessional behaviour that prevailed in the goods businesses.

The stock market, on the other hand, could give him the privilege to trade from anywhere in the world and without talking to anyone—no begging, no bad debts, no dead inventory, no liquidation problem, and no scalability issues. These were just a few things he would be happy to leave behind. So the trader taught him everything about the markets—why prices moved up and down, how not to get carried away by the ever-moving price ticker, and to look at the bigger picture. Then, he started teaching him about the basics of technical analysis right from scratch—candle sticks to indicators and advanced strategies.

Rahul did his homework with total dedication and even started to take an interest in stock market books and watched many videos online. He knew deep inside that he had already found his chosen path and could do this for the rest of his life. So he visited the trader a few more times that month and soaked in all the information he possibly could.

Not everyone shares their knowledge freely, and he was grateful to the trader who had become his mentor and taught him a lot of new things every day. Once Rahul felt confident that he had acquired the knowledge to trade successfully in the markets, he took his first trade. He followed one of the strategies his mentor had taught him, and, you guessed it right, he made a good profit from it.

Rahul felt a sense of satisfaction that his hard work had already started to deliver results. He had invested a small amount as he was new to the markets and wanted to get a feel for it before jumping in with full momentum. Almost every trade he took made money, and he was on top of the world. He could not believe that it was so easy to make money in the markets, and he even suggested trading in the stock market to his family members. What he did not realise was that he had entered in a soaring bull market, and his dream run was about to end. After making a few small gains, he decided to pump in more capital, start making a decent amount of money off the markets, and leave his family business altogether.

As soon as he started trading a much bigger account, he began to lose money because he was not mentally prepared to handle a bigger account. Rahul was about to learn about position sizing the hard way. He got stuck in a trade, and instead of booking out for a small loss, he tried averaging because he had only seen his stocks go up and believed that this time would be no different.

Rahul kept trying to average on every major fall, but his ego did not allow him to exit with a loss. Eventually, he exited with a much bigger loss. It frustrated him that most of the money he made while trading his small account was lost in a single trade. He felt angry that the stock market had taken something from him and wanted his money back quickly! He kept losing more money trying to recover his previous loss. The very strategies that had made him money earlier now seemed to betray him. However, he was astute enough to figure out that it was not his strategies at fault but his own emotions.

The harder he tried to recover his losses, the more they increased. He desperately wanted his hard-earned money back and even tried to put in more money in every trade to see if it would better his chances of recovering the money he lost. Before he knew it, he had blown most of the money in his account. It was a shock, and he promised himself that he would recover his losses. This time, he would lay down a plan, follow it and even study his previous trades to find out what went wrong.

Rahul took a break from the markets for a few months and went back to studying—he spent hours every day reviewing his past mistakes. It led him to focus on other aspects of trading, such as position sizing, risk management, and, last but not least, the psychology of a successful trader. He read many books on psychology and mindset and started trading again after a few months—this time well prepared. He gradually increased his position size, modified his trading approach, and eventually made it big. He continues to trade for a living and enjoy his life. Surprise! This is actually my story—Rahul was just a pseudonym.

We all want to enjoy the lifestyle that a trader enjoys—he is his own boss, can work according to his convenience, does not have to travel daily to work and can practically work from anywhere in the world. There are thousands of benefits of being a full-time trader and investor, but it needs practice and study to excel in it, like any other business.

In the following chapters, I will explain the critical factors that should be followed, with the hope that they will help you in your trading journey as much as they helped in mine.

02

KNOW YOURSELF FIRST

THANK YOU, STOCK MARKET, FOR TEACHING ME SO MUCH ABOUT MYSELF.
I NEVER KNEW IT WOULD BE THIS WAY ROUND!

Rahul did everything that he could to learn about the markets and how they work, but he never tried to know how his mind works, which is crucial in the market. If only studying the aspects of markets could be enough, all chartered accountants and chartered market technicians would have been successful in the market. But that is not the case.

It is imperative to know how

- you *think*
- you *process information*
- you *react to a loss*
- you *react after a profit*
- you *control our ego*
- *easily excitable you are*

These aspects are essential and lay special emphasis on your own thought processes. Psychology plays a huge role in the success or failure of a trader. You can learn about the technical or fundamental aspects of the markets in a few days, but it can take a lifetime to understand how your own mind works.

Your mind is like a powerful machine—it can work with you or against you, depending on how you use it.

Only if you know how your mind and thought process work or what "fuels" it can you work on yourself. You need to fight the "enemies"—*krodh* (anger), *lobh* (greed), *moh* (attachment), *ahankaara* (ego)—to gain control. These are present in all aspects of life, and the ultimate motive is to win over them and not be binded by them throughout your life.

To prosper, you really need to take charge of yourself and make sure that you are not affected. For example, in markets, if you get angry, you might feel frustrated after a loss, despite knowing that it is a part of the process and it will always be there.

Your job is to make sure that you have your

losses in control. The amount that you are willing to lose should be pre-decided and not calculated according to your emotions while you are in a trade. After a loss, the previous trade appears more significant as soon as you take the next trade. The anger could lead to revenge trading to cover up the losses as soon as possible, which may cause more losses if you trade irrationally without calculating according to the technical setup or risk-reward ratio, just to recover the previous loss. In most cases, you may just be so desperate to get your money back that you end up losing more of it. I have seen many traders getting angry and frustrated and then try to recover their losses on the same day as if the market would not open the next day.

I have even seen people trading in the same stock as if the stock has memory and it knows that it has taken some money from your pocket and now it is liable to pay it back to you. Avoid going into such a situation if you learn to forgive yourself and understand that this is a game of probability, and that you do not have to be correct every time. We just have to be correct *big* and wrong *small*. So having control over *krodh* is essential.

The next aspect is *lobh* or greed. It is one of the most critical aspects, and if you do not know how to control it, you may never be successful in trading. Again, technical setups or fundamental reasons are essential, but they will not matter if you do not control your greed.

Trading is mainly about how much control you have over greed. When you make a profit, you may get greedy and try to book it as soon as you see it on the screen, only to realise that if you had held it long enough, you would not have made much more.

This greed works in other ways too. For example, when you face a loss, your greed makes you hold on to it, hoping that you would eventually recover it someday in the future. Unfortunately, in most cases, the loss keeps getting bigger and bigger before you realise your mistake and have already booked a significant loss.

So, greed is one of the most important factors you should know how to control if you really want to be successful in the stock market. I always tell my friends—be happy for your profit instead of yearning for the extra profit that you could have made. Whatever happens, happens for the good.

A simple hack that I use to control my greed is that I simply remove the stock from my watchlist as soon as I exit the stock. After booking my profit, there is no point in looking at it again and again on that same day because it would either go up or down. If it goes up, you will regret exiting it. Or if it goes down, you may be tempted to buy it again just to replicate the move. But this time, it could come down after getting rejected at resistance and may not take support. You might end up losing your previous profit and even some of your capital.

The next aspect is *moh* or attachment. When you study a lot about a company, you sometimes go into very minute details and get attached to it. At times, you may get so attached that you do not ever think about exiting from that stock even if it hits your stop-loss. A thorough study of any company or any subject is a good thing; what I am saying is that we should be open-minded regarding our investments and not get attached to them.

A mistake that I repeatedly made during the initial trading years was that I always entered a trade according to the technical aspects or indications on the chart, but once the stock came closer to my stop-loss, I would jump on to the fundamental aspects of the company just to assure myself that the company was sound and would be able to recover some day.

This was wrong because I had made a plan to exit at a specific price when I entered, and when the stock finally reached that level, I should not deviate from the plan just because I got attached to the trade. I know some stocks can rebound and again come into profit, but there are hundreds of examples of stocks that have become penny stocks or even delisted. People lose their entire capital because of their attachment to a company, so much so that they bet their entire capital on that particular stock and keep on averaging it at every significant dip.

Our religious scriptures have always advised detachment from as many things as possible. That is why the saints and sadhus would go to the Himalayas to meditate. In a way, they were detaching themselves from a busy life and worldly possessions.

The next aspect is *ahankaara* or ego. We all know that ego can be really dangerous for any kind of business or life. It is said that in a war of egos, the loser always wins. Inevitably, the more knowledge you have about a subject, the lesser ego you will have.

The stock market is a great place to see people generally begin with inflated egos. Once they see the cycles of ups and downs—and most traders and investors have blown up their capital at least once even before they come to know about the market—they tend to lose their ego, and realise that the stock market is an ocean and we are just a tiny drop.

Let us look at the super successful investors like Warren Buffet, Charlie Munger, Peter Lynch, Ramdeo Agrawal, Rakesh Jhunjhunwala, Radhakishan Damani, etc. I have had the honour of meeting a few of these big names personally, and was blown away by their humility and soft-spoken nature. One reason could be that almost all of them came from very humble backgrounds and learnt so much from the markets that they never let ego get in the way.

It is imperative to have the discipline and patience to control all these emotions to excel in the stock market or any other profession.

PROFIT

03

DO YOU HAVE A PRO-TRADER'S MINDSET?

A TRADER SHOULD WORK VERY HARD PREPARING THEIR TRADES, BUT THEIR ACTUAL TRADING SHOULD BE EFFORTLESS.

You enter the market with a vision of getting rich overnight and make a killing in the markets. You assume that it is effortless to make money here, and start trading from day one without acquiring any knowledge. Once you face reality, probably after a few losses, you realise that you need to learn about this. Then you start learning about the technical or fundamental studies which are the most critical aspects of the market as they are the basics of chart reading. But, the mind is the tool that puts any study into use, and it is really important to focus on it first.

Therefore, you should be well acquainted with these basics before setting out on the journey of successful trading. However, a trader's mindset should be given much more importance as it decides how a trader will perform and manage trades.

You can learn about the technical aspects of trading by following the traditional approach of reading books or by taking guidance from teachers and mentors. What is really difficult is understanding the mindset—you are not aware of how to do it, and were never taught about it in school or college.

The journey is a very long and laborious one, but that is what trading is all about. Most successful traders are really passionate so they enjoy the journey and realise that money is a by-product of good trading.

It is not easy to master the mind, but there is no other option. You have to know how to use it efficiently to make it work for you and not against you. To do this, you can follow these easy steps:

1. **Write down the plan *before* taking the trade:** This may seem like a very basic thing to do, but most people skip this part. It is essential to write down your plan *before* taking the trade. Once you have a written plan, with well-defined

entry, exit, position size and reason for the entry, and most importantly, exit, you take care of any anxiety by creating a well-structured plan. The next step is just to sit back and execute the plan. I have observed that a written plan takes care of most of the fretting that you may develop once you are in the trade.

2. **Too much information:** Earlier, there was very little information available regarding companies listed on the stock market. People would hunt for any information that they could lay their hands on about the company in which they had invested or the stock price of the company they were interested in. They would get stock prices by going to the broker's office or from the newspapers. Unfortunately, most traders did not have the real-time prices.

   These days, however, this information is abundantly available, making it confusing to decide what is actually important. You can get overwhelmed with the volume of information available out there, and it eventually makes you deviate from your plan.

With business channels which run 24x7 and provide free stock recommendations, traders and analysts giving their views on social media, it is challenging to remain sane and be able to distinguish between useful information from all the data at your disposal.

Many of my trader friends and I do not watch business channels at all. We do not log on to social media during market hours either. Most people I follow on social media are my friends and they do not give any stock suggestions. This helps me focus only on my analysis, irrespective of what the world out there is doing.

It is easy to say that you do not get carried away with other's opinions. However, when someone's contrary view about your trade lingers at the back of your mind, you tend to get worried if that particular stock starts moving against you. It may make you think, "what if that guy knows much more than me?" or "Did I really take a good decision by entering into this trade?"

3. **It is a probability game:** Trading is a game of probabilities, and I have often said, "whenever

you make a loss, you should not take it to heart, and if you make a profit, you should not take it to your mind!" Both these situations negatively impact your mind, and you are bound to make irrational decisions as you move ahead.

It is a fact that you should not trade with ego. If you make a loss, do not feel bad, punish yourself, or doubt your abilities. The purpose is to keep making good trades and not to think much about the monetary reward.

Remember that the trade that you are taking is just 1 of the next 1000 trades you are going to take. Do not get so emotionally attached to it that you end up losing your sleep if it does not go according to plan. By minimising the importance of that one trade, you can proceed with ease and would be in a better frame of mind to take sound decisions.

Almost all professional traders use these techniques to stay one step ahead of the rest. However, with years of experience, they realise the importance of controlling the mind. Trading is a serious profession that needs to be carried out with a proper plan and not just with a hit-and-run approach.

04

THE THREE MONKEYS

IF YOU CANNOT CONVERT 10,000 TO 20,000, YOU SHOULD NOT TRY TO CONVERT 1,00,000 TO 2,00,000

Have you ever wondered why there are thousands or maybe millions of traders who have never been profitable but still keep trading? Even after all this time, if they still cannot make consistent profits from the market, they should have realised many years ago that something was wrong in their approach towards the markets. But instead of working towards profitability, they end up trading even more aggressively, losing more money, and the cycle continues. So it actually has got a lot to do with the wiring of your brain.

There was an experiment conducted with three monkeys in which they were supposed to do a similar task, but were rewarded unequally.

The first monkey was instructed to do a task, and

as soon as he completed it, he was given a reward. He repeated the task and again got the prize. He now knew that he would be rewarded every time he completed the task, so he kept on doing it until he was exhausted and decided to wait for a while.

The second monkey was also instructed to complete the same task, but did not get any reward. He got confused and did the task again as he expected a reward similar to the one given to the first monkey. But there was no reward given. He soon realised that whatever he was doing was in vain, so he stopped immediately and did not show any further interest in the task, even when the instructors told him to do it again. The instructors tried to force him to do the task, but he still would not do it as he knew by now that there was no reward attached to the task.

The third monkey was rewarded differently. He was rewarded on random occasions—on the first attempt, on the third, then on the fifth and sixth attempt, and then directly on the ninth attempt. He received rewards, but at uncertain intervals. So since the monkey did not know when the reward would come and when it would not, he kept on doing the task every time in the hope that he would definitely get the reward sometime.

This uncertain rewarding system made him do the task every single time till he too got exhausted, just like the first monkey. But in this case, he got very few rewards compared to the first monkey.

You can see the similarities in this style of getting rewards with trading. As it relies on probability, in trading too, you get rewards at uncertain intervals. You may get a winning streak or a losing streak, but the rewards from these trades is generally uncertain.

In the initial days of trading, when you get good profits, you end up thinking that maybe this will continue forever, and when it does not, you continue trading in the hope of similar results. Similar results may be attained again, and they may come anytime, but the hope makes you trade again and again even if the first few profits were just out of luck. The market is constructed in a way that you know you cannot profit from each and every trade, but still expect to profit from each trade you take. So you attach your hopes and get excited about every trade.

A hormone called dopamine has a role to play in this type of behaviour. It is a feel-good hormone, and our brain craves it. Whenever the monkeys get the reward, or whenever you get profits, this hormone is released in excess throughout your body, and your brain tells you that it liked whatever just happened and wants more of it. This craving and greed for more of this rush makes you keep repeating the action, even if the reward is collected randomly.

It is one of the reasons why traders who blow up their entire capital still keep on trading. They even go to the extent of borrowing money from friends and relatives just to trade. Eventually, they get so addicted to the random reward that they just cannot let it go. Trading becomes so addictive to them that they sometimes even end up losing the borrowed money and then go into depression.

So it is essential to know why you overtrade and how to overcome this, using some of the hacks and tricks I have tried to explain in this book.

ZZZ

05

THE THREE SALESMEN

A SERIES OF PROFITS MAKE US GREEDY AND A SERIES OF LOSSES MAKE US FEARFUL.

TAKING A SMALL BREAK AFTER BOTH THESE SCENARIOS HELPS A LOT.

After the story of the three monkeys, let me tell you another story.

There was a shop that had three salesmen. The first one was very obedient, and he would talk very politely with all customers. He would attend to their demands and was very dear to the shop owner as well. He had a charming personality and was great at bargaining too; he never let any of the customers leave the shop empty-handed. All loved him, and he proved to be one of the best salesmen the shop owner had ever had. Since he got employed at the shop, he had immensely benefitted it, and the owner made huge profits because of him.

The second salesman was a decent guy but a lazy one. He would not talk politely with customers, neither did he speak rudely. He would just sit idly in the shop. He was neither a burden nor an asset to the shop. He would just sit idle and mind his own business most of the time. The shopkeeper did not fire him in the hopes that he may turn into a good salesman one day.

Then there was a third salesman. He was very rude to the customers and was always angry. He had very little patience and was always ready to fight with every customer. Customers literally tried to avoid any contact with him as they knew of his temper and attitude. The shopkeeper was also annoyed with him and knew that he was just a liability to the shop and had never been beneficial. He did not generate any profits for the shop and had driven away many customers with his attitude and rude behaviour. Everyone was upset with him as he created a very negative ambience in the shop. He behaved rudely with his co-workers, customers, and the shop owner as well.

One day, because of reduced sales, the shopkeeper had to fire one of the salesmen, as he literally could not afford three salespeople. What do you think the shopkeeper did? Which salesman would have been fired? The third one, right? I am pretty sure there is no doubt about that.

And that is what happened. The shopkeeper fired the third salesman as it was obvious that he was no good to the shop and was just a burden on everyone. The shopkeeper felt relieved as soon as he fired him because it allowed him to save some money. He would not need to worry about someone talking rudely to his customers now, and the other two salesmen were also very happy that they could perform their duty even more efficiently.

Now let us relate this story with the stock market.

Suppose you have three open positions in your demat account. The first position is giving significant profits, and is basically in an uptrend. It has been giving substantial gains since it was purchased as the uptrend was just starting, and the trend was still very strong. There was no reversal sign in sight, and it was clear that it could be held in the portfolio for much longer. In technical terms, it was making 'higher highs and higher lows', was above the important moving averages, and was strong in the relative strength indicator. To cut a long story short, it was the perfect stock that anyone could have in their portfolio.

There was the second stock, which performed just like the second salesman. It was at breakeven—not giving any profit, nor any loss. Since the day that stock was bought, it just lay there near the purchase value. It was neither a burden to the trader nor an asset. It waited for the next move. As it was just lying there, it did not bother the trader much and he could focus on his routine work, finding new stocks, looking for new sectors to trade, etc.

Then there was the third stock, which had been incurring losses since you bought it. It was a burden as it took money from the account, but instead of exiting it, you keep holding it in the hope that it 'may' recover sometime in the future.

Your behaviour is totally irrational when dealing in the stock market, and it can take a lot of time, experience, and losses until you realise what you have been doing.

Traders have many stocks in their portfolios. So whenever a stock gives good moves on the upside and shows some profits, traders get eager to sell it and close the position. In simple words, they are impatient with the profitable stocks.

At the same time, when a stock starts falling, they recall all the Warren Buffet quotes regarding patience, and hold these bleeding stocks for many years.

As a trader, have you experienced this?

Can you think of any correlation between the story of the three salespeople and portfolio holdings?

Your guess is correct! The same thought process influenced your decision-making, and most of you end up selling profitable stocks soon. It is the first mistake. Besides, most people end up holding all the losing stocks. It is the second mistake.

A trader or investor will become successful only if he reverses the equation, that is, as traders, we should be impatient with the losing trades, and be patient with the winning trades.

JACKPOT
777

06

MRI SCANS OF GAMBLERS

1 SIMPLE STRATEGY AND A CALM MIND IS BETTER THAN 100 INDICATORS!

This may be one of the most interesting things you will ever read about gamblers. In fact, traders who act like gamblers are under the illusion that they are in perfect control of their emotions.

There was a study done by a cognitive neuroscientist named Reza Habib. It was a study on 30 gamblers. Of these, 15 were compulsive gamblers, that is, they had an addiction to gambling and could not control themselves. The other 15 were social gamblers—they only gambled once in a while and were okay with losing a few bucks and exiting the casino to reduce their loss.

Reza Habib looked at the scans of both groups of gamblers (compulsive gamblers and social gamblers) while they looked at a slot machine. In a slot machine, you can either get a win, a loss, or a near miss. Interestingly, compulsive gamblers' brains showed much more activity when they won or had a near miss. In fact, they treated the near miss as a win. They thought that they were so close to winning in the case of a near win that they got the same shot of dopamine as they would have when they actually won. So even though they lost virtual money in the case of a near miss, they still treated it as if they had won.

Now remember, there was no money involved—it was just a simulation—and yet, they got excited, which could clearly be seen in their brain scans in real time. This is the reason why these kinds of gamblers keep playing for so long—they are basically unable to stop themselves. Each near miss feels as if they actually won. This hope keeps them hooked to play more, desperate to actually win.

When the second group was studied, which comprised the 15 social gamblers, they behaved normally. They treated the near misses as what they were—a loss. It does not matter if you lost by a margin or lost by a near miss, a loss is a loss. The area of their brain that shows the activation of dopamine did not light up. When they had a few near misses, they realised that if they kept losing money like this, they would eventually go broke, and they stopped playing. This awareness was completely missing in the compulsive gamblers.

This is true in the case of trading too. You would have seen addicted traders, who may be trading options or intraday without any plan. Just for the thrill of it, they display the same characteristics. (I am not saying that all option and intraday players are addicted, but there are many who play without any rules, just like compulsive gamblers do.) When these traders get a near miss, or when they notice that they booked out of a trade that could have given them 10–20 times returns, they get a shot of dopamine. They get excited and realise that they were so close to making a fortune, and swear to themselves that next time, whenever a similar trade comes up, they will go in with full force. They end up losing their capital, drop by drop, in the hope of that "next time." They get so addicted because they have almost tasted huge success. I have seen many traders who lost their entire capital, their life savings, borrowed capital from their family members and friends, lost that too, and still try to arrange funds from somewhere so that they may finally hit that jackpot trade they missed.

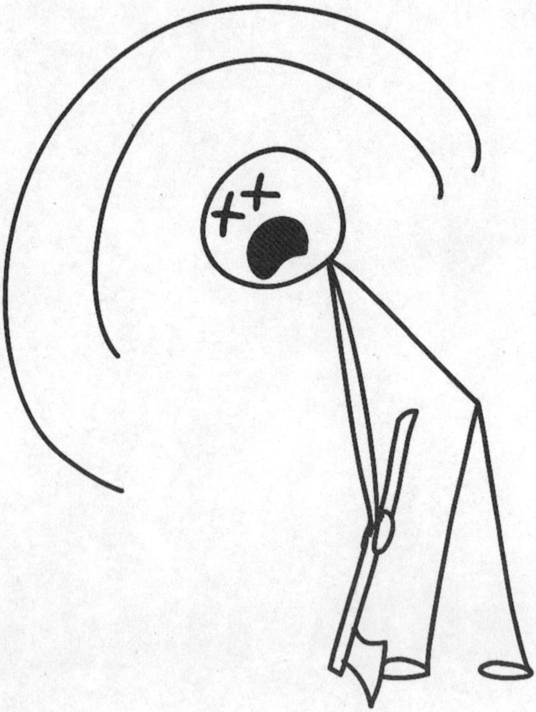

07

YOU ARE THE REASON FOR YOUR LOSSES

A STRATEGY WILL NOT SAVE YOU IF YOUR MINDSET IS BROKEN. YOU WILL STILL OVERTRADE, PANIC, AND FORCE SETUPS. FIX THE INNER TRADER FIRST.

It is really easy to trade profitably. Yes, I know that is not what you may have heard. But most of the pitfalls that you fall into are self-created. Yes, you are the weakest link in your trading world—the biggest obstacle to your own trading success. To improve your trading, you need to identify and fix your weaknesses. By overcomplicating your process, you are unable to execute the trades flawlessly when the right time comes.

Here are a few ways in which you may become your own enemy in the process of profitable trading:

1. You have a tendency to micro-manage your trades

You may tell yourself that you watch only higher time frame charts like the daily and weekly, but end up checking on the market every five minutes. You are so curious to know how your stocks are performing that you are unable to let them do their thing. You may think that if you do not watch them consistently, they may crash. If you watch your stocks every five minutes, then you are not following the daily charts—you are actually checking the 5-minute charts. The problem with this approach is that we get many signals according to the 5-minute chart. As the candle closes every 5 minutes, you may start seeing some chart patterns, breakouts or breakdowns, and panic and exit your positions, which may work really well according to the higher time frame charts. Many times in your trading career you may have exited a position without any reason and when you realised your mistake, the stock may have already run up a lot from there, and you could not enter it again. Now that stock will be in your "I wish I held that stock longer" list.

Sometimes, even if you do not check the charts every 5 minutes, you check your profit and loss screen regularly. It may seem harmless, but what it is actually doing is creating patterns in your subconscious mind.

Imagine you have a running position and you are currently at a profit of 10,000. After some time, you check that the profit has increased to a total of 15,000. You feel really happy and content with your trade. Sometime later, you notice that the profit is now only 8,000 and further drops to just 7,000. Technically speaking, the trend on the higher time frame charts may remain intact, and there would be no need to panic at all. But since you have seen this journey from 15,000 to 7,000, you panic. Now, if the profit comes back to even 10,000 again, you will thank the stock market lords for it and exit instantly. That stock might just be entering a great uptrend rally. It might move up so much from that point that you regret your exit decision and just watch that stock soaring up like a rocket. You will feel that you missed out, causing regret, frustration, and whatnot, because you exited it too early. All this happened because you were too concerned and obsessed with your profit and loss screen.

That is why I always say that screen time is a

friend for an intraday trader, but a brutal enemy for a swing trader. The reason I am able to manage making videos for my YouTube channel and Instagram, write books, work on my health, and much more is because I watch the daily charts. I essentially have to check my positions just for a few minutes in the morning and then for a few minutes before the market closes, not throughout the day.

2. You over-analyse and do not actually execute

Ideally, you should learn a few strategies and then try them out and see what works for you. There is no perfect strategy. But you end up looking for that holy grail throughout your trading careers.

Look for a strategy that suits your lifestyle, risk appetite and temperament. Once you find it, stick to it religiously. You will learn along the way as you execute a lot of trades. You may go into so much depth about the strategy that you even go into the calculations of how the strategy is derived, what calculations are going on in real-time, who invented it, etc. Remember, you have to trade and make money from the markets—you do not have to write a thesis.

Each and every loss-making trade teaches you so much more than any book out there ever will. But most people do not execute enough, and do not stick to a strategy long enough to actually know what works and what does not. They never actually sit down with their trading journal and observe what needs to be stopped, or what they need to double down on and give more emphasis to. They always get carried away by the latest influencer who shouts at the top of his voice, telling viewers to try their strategy which has a 99.9% accuracy. Most people never realise that the issues they are facing in trading are a result of their own behaviour and psychological issues—not about the strategy. Strategy is a very small part of the trading equation. If you observe the best—and in fact, the legendary—traders out there, you will always observe that their charts are clean (no fancy indicators or just 1–2 basic indicators).

Simple strategies like the 20-moving average, super trend, relative strength indicator (RSI), etc., work well if you want to trail your profits or want to know where to exit if something goes against the trend. You do not need much more than this.

3. You trade out of FOMO, greed, and fear

How can you actually not trade out of fear of missing out, greed, and fear? It is emotions that make us human, but you have been told not to trade with emotions. The only solution to this is to have a checklist that tells you everything. It functions as your lighthouse that guides you through storms of emotions. When you feel stuck, weighed down by these emotions, having a clear, straightforward, and robust checklist will make all the difference. This is what separates an amateur trader from a professional one.

In the checklist, include all the things you need to verify before entering a trade along with a clear exit strategy. Most traders just enter a trade out of excitement and hope. They only think about the exit once they are already in the trade. That is not a wise thing to do. You need to think and make decisions prior to entering into a position. A checklist can be as simple as having a criterion for the minimum market cap of a company.

For example, your checklist could include rules which state the following:

- Never enter a trade if the market capitalisation of the company is less than Rs 500 crore.
- Never enter a trade if the stock's price is trading below the 200-moving average on the daily chart. The 200-moving average is like the backbone of a chart. If that is broken, do not even touch that stock till it starts trading above it. In fact, it would be even better to trade in stocks that are trading above their important moving averages like 20-moving average and 50-moving average, which indicates that the stock is in an uptrend and has momentum.

Once you follow a momentum checklist, you will see a lot of probable trades on your scanners during an up-trending market. You may feel that there are so many opportunities but not enough funds to trade them. During sideways and choppy markets, when there is no trend, there may come a time when you do not take a single trade for days or even weeks. That is the best part of checklists—you trade according to the market condition and your rules, not your emotions.

If you want to trade seriously as a business, you need to have a structure. Otherwise, you will just end up taking random trades and switching your strategy every other day—and that is not called trading but gambling. Whenever you take decisions out of fear and not from a plan, it will always be a bad one—and this is not true just for markets, but for life too.

4. Revenge Trading

As the saying goes, "Don't take your profits to your head and your losses to your heart." Losses are a part of the game—they are the cost of running this business, and are a routine part of a trader's life. You cannot run away from them. Take the losses gracefully and cut them while they are small so that you are able to take the next trade. There is no need to take losses to your ego and feel bad about them. Many traders cannot accept the fact that you just need to have a win ratio of 50–55% to be a profitable trader. Most people who may be quite successful in other careers end up being awful traders because they cannot accept being wrong.

If you are a doctor, you need to have as much accuracy as possible—that is what is expected in your profession. So, when you start trading, it may be difficult to fathom the fact that it's okay to be wrong almost half the time and still win big. This is the holy grail of trading—the secret that everyone is looking for. Risk management is the only secret here.

As long as you manage your losses by taking them early and small—and you are able to ride your profits as long as the trailing stop-loss is not hit (which can be calculated in a number of ways like following moving averages, super trend, MACD, etc.)—you will eventually make a lot of money in this profession.

Most problems in trading are created by your own mind. You unnecessarily make trading so complicated that you run out of willpower and capital after some time, and just quit and call it gambling. You hardly admit the fact that it is not about the profession, but how we look at and treat it.

08

CAN TRADING BE PEACEFUL?

A TRADER WITHOUT A PLAN IS JUST A GAMBLER WITH A SCREEN.

Trading—and that too, peaceful? Do you really think about how to make your trading peaceful? Or do you just want to maximise your returns and profits? Do you just want the highest return on investment (ROI) at the cost of peace?

Think about it for a moment: how many times have you thought about peace when you think about trading?

Usually, peace and trading are never used in a single sentence, ever. Traders are either shown as people who are very stressed and sitting in front of the terminal all day long. Or, they are shown enjoying their luxury cars, trading off the beaches, and just swimming in pools of money. I find it funny that people leave their jobs to become traders as they may have felt suffocated in their jobs and wanted to do something different, something that they could love and enjoy. But they end up treating trading as an even more stressful endeavour compared to their job—sitting in front of the trading terminal all day long. Trading is a lonely job, and they end up isolating themselves from their friends and peers and spend most of their time at their trading desks. They watch the world news as if everything depends on it. They watch the world markets and want to know whatever is happening out there—as if they can change it. Traders also end up trading multiple asset classes rather than sticking to only one or two that actually suit them.

I have seen traders trading the Indian markets, then checking the crypto markets in the afternoon, and trading the US markets in the evening till midnight. Worst of all, they end up waking up abruptly from sleep in the middle of the night to check how the forex markets are doing!

This is not what they signed up for, and we need to do something about it.

To make trading peaceful, you need to have

realistic expectations, and you need to align your goals with them. So, following these steps, you can become a peaceful trader:

1. Have realistic expectations

Most people usually enter the markets with unrealistic expectations, and that is not completely their fault. They are led to believe that it is completely normal to make millions from the market in a few months, influenced by social media. Influencers show off their profits and lifestyle—people who might have a vested interest in showing off to you. Most people are not even comfortable sharing how much they earn with their close relatives. Then there are influencers on social media, showing off their millions in profits to thousands of followers—who are basically strangers.

It is not that those traders are not making that kind of money—they might be—but when someone keeps showing off their profits and lifestyle so openly to strangers, there is usually a hidden agenda behind it. Most likely they want to sell their services, and there is nothing wrong with selling services or digital products. But showing off or projecting a false image of something just so that they can sell their services quickly is misleading. You never know what kind of image you imprint in the minds of followers who watch you on social media. I have heard so many stories of people quitting their stable jobs to become full-time traders. They do not even set aside an emergency fund, and just jump into full-time trading because they have been served the illusion that full-time trading is the easiest thing out there.

Now, if you have been trading for some time, you know how difficult it can be to make a living out of trading. You have to fight with your emotions on a daily basis. You have to grow as a person to become a better trader. You need to build systems that can separate emotional thinking from your decisions. Moreover, trading is a business—you will not get monthly returns here. You might have a few amazing months when you make a lot of money, and there might be periods of sideways movement where you hardly make anything. These are the times when you will be tested—when you get thoughts of quitting. But a person who enters the markets with realistic expectations will surf these waves of confusion with ease. A person who enters the markets with the right expectations and approach will sit patiently during these tough times and will not panic.

2. Make the trading process easy

People overcomplicate the process of trading. You think that it has to be complex for it to work. You cannot wrap your head around the fact that something easy can be profitable too. When a new trader enters the market, they think they need to work very hard to make it work—which is true—but only for the initial months or years while they are learning the process. Once you have figured out the strategy and style of trading that suits you, take it easy. Do minimal work to get maximum returns then. You do not need to complicate your trading with fancy indicators. Neither do you need to use a lot of indicators—more does not mean better here. If you apply too many indicators, you will always remain confused, as one indicator may tell you to buy, whereas another may signal you to sell. Most of the time, basic support and resistance levels work equally well. Indicators are eventually derived from the basic price action itself. Yes, it is also true that to come to these simple setups, you need to learn a few indicators—but you do not need to stick with them forever.

3. Choose your battlefield

When you enter the markets, you are lured toward intraday trading. Because, why not? If someone had the option of getting profits the same day, who would not love it? Who wants to wait for months and years to book profits? But you need to evaluate whether a style of trading matches your mindset, temperament, and nature. Someone might make decent money in intraday, but it may be the worst style of trading for you. I have seen traders who stick to intraday for 3–4 years without making any profits. They eventually break even and then make 12–15% annually. Their lives are messed up as they hardly have time or energy for anything else after trading aggressively throughout trading hours. I would advise them to just invest their money in mutual funds if they want these kinds of returns. There is no use taking so much pain for average returns in the first place. I think traders also understand this, but they are addicted to trading and are not able to leave it. The urge to do something all the time has taken over.

Another thing you may notice if you trade consistently on shorter time frames is that you will feel frustrated and irritated all the time. If your family member calls you or your friend calls during market hours, you could get impatient and just prefer to get back to trading the markets. This is a clear sign of addiction, which traders might not realise initially. Even on weekends, you will think about the markets. You will not be able to wait for Monday when you can finally get a chance to punch another trade.

Now, this is not a sustainable way to live. Most traders entered markets because they were not happy with their jobs. They wanted a better lifestyle, to grow as a person and feel more satisfied—but they end up making their lives even more miserable by trading this way.

4. Try a better type of trading

In the initial years at least, try swing or positional trading. In fact, I would urge everyone to stick to higher time frame trading, as that would suit 99% of traders out there. It is not compulsory that we do all types of trading. Swing trading is when you take a trade for more than one day and keep it for a few days or weeks till the trend is intact. Positional trading is similar, but you look to ride the trends for even longer—like following the weekly charts. The stop-loss would be bigger in this case, but once you catch a nice trend, the profits will be much bigger. A single profitable trade can sometimes take care of 8–10 stop-losses—that is the power of trading higher time frames.

The best part is that you can focus on other elements of your life along with swing trading and positional trading, as you do not need to be glued to your trading terminal all day long. In fact, you would get better results if you stay away from the screen and focus on other things. I often get messages on social media from traders who were making decent returns from swing trading, but tried options trading and lost a lot of money. They ask me how to deal with it. My simple reply is that if they have already figured out that swing trading suits them, then they should just stick to it. There is no need to jump to options or futures trading. Just do the stuff that you are good at—you do not have to do everything.

I have been doing swing trading for almost a decade now, and that is the reason I am able to take out time for other things like posting content on Instagram, YouTube, etc. Even during market hours I write and read multiple books as I literally have a lot of time. I am even able to take care of my health and go to the gym during trading hours very easily. In fact, during market hours, I am usually sitting in a park and reading books—something I always wished for but could not do while running my traditional family business.

Just checking the markets for a few minutes in the morning and then a few minutes near closing time is all I need to trade better—and peacefully. You can even journal your trades easily and look for patterns to understand what is working and where you need to improve—which is almost impossible to do if you trade intraday and multiple times a day.

NAM

09

NEVER OVERTRADE AGAIN

THE MARKET
REFLECTS YOUR
STATE OF MIND.

IF YOU ARE
CHAOTIC INSIDE,
YOUR TRADES
WILL BE TOO.

Overtrading is the most important topic for any trader. Most new traders find themselves overtrading before they even know it, and end up wiping out their entire capital, only to regret it later. Even experienced traders sometimes end up overtrading and lose their entire gains, and even a major part of their capital, if they do not stop it before it's too late. Almost 90% of the messages I get on my social media profiles are related to overtrading, which explains why this is such an important topic to address.

There are two types of traders who overtrade. The first type are traders who do not even know that they are overtrading, and that causes them all the frustration, losses, and anxiety.

The second type are traders who do not know that the main cause of their poor trading results is overtrading. They do not even realise that they are overtrading and they feel that their trading style and frequency are completely normal because that is how they have seen their idols and social media influencers trade (or pretend to trade).

Let us discuss some of the major solutions for overtrading. If you really follow these steps, I assure you that you will never overtrade again and you will not feel anxious every time you trade.

1. Have a maximum loss limit

You never know the upside of a stock, but you can and should always fix the downside. This is the most important trait of legendary traders; they know when to cut their losses and move on to the next trade. They do not marry a trade. They are ready to move on to the next one if something is not working well. If you trade intraday, have a maximum loss limit for the day. For example, if you fix that your maximum loss limit is Rs 5000, then exit as soon as this number is hit. Do not wait for another trade to recover your loss. We all know how that ends. Just shut down the trading terminal and get up right away.

When you see that you have already reached your loss limit—in this case, 5000—and you try to recover it, you may lose another 5000 or even more. You end up taking a lot of trades just to recover this amount. You enter this revenge mode and just make the broker rich by punching hundreds of trades to recover. By the end of the day, you will realise that you were not able to recover. In fact, you ended up losing more and took a lot of trades, which resulted in more losses in the way of brokerage and transaction costs, and you even end up totally exhausted by the end of the trading day. You will feel frustrated and will not have the energy to do anything else that day. You might just think about the next trading day, since you have already faced a loss and still want to recover. You might feel that the market is rigged against you and some operator or big player is hitting your stop-losses. So, instead of going through all this pain, it is always better to just follow this basic rule and exit when the maximum loss limit hits.

This way, you will not end up taking hundreds of trades and will, in fact, have the time and mental clarity to check what went wrong. You can journal your trades in the evening that day and see your mistakes and how you can improve in the next trade.

2. Follow "Trading Detox"

I discussed this point in one of my YouTube videos, and a lot of traders really liked this idea and even promised to follow it.

You might have heard about digital detox, where one does not use their mobiles and social media apps, and takes a break to rejuvenate themselves. It is like a reset to our digital consumption habits. Trading detox works in the same way for trading. You have to take a break from trading for one week. You do not even have to check the index (Nifty, Bank Nifty, etc.). You do not even have to follow market news—no news on TV or reading business newspapers. One week of complete market detox.

I know it might sound a bit harsh, but this is needed, and traders end up getting to know about their patterns by the end of this detox. They get to know their own shortcomings and behaviours which they would never have noticed if they did not take the detox. What will happen in the first and second days of the detox is that you might get a strong urge to check your portfolio or the general market prices. You will feel the urge to check your phone multiple times out of habit. You might feel that you are missing a lot. This pattern reveals how addicted you may be to checking the prices multiple times in a day. This may not help your trading in any way, but you still might have this habit of re-checking the prices all the time throughout the trading hours. You get a kind of dopamine hit whenever you see numbers going up and down. A small profit in your portfolio can increase your greed and you might want to see the profit rising. A small loss might give you the hope that the price may recover and we may see a profit and feel good again.

Over the next few days of the detox, you may realise that you were so addicted to checking the prices and that you need to do something about this habit.

In the last couple of days of the trading detox week, traders generally sit with pen and paper and journal their thoughts. They write down what they learned in this detox week. This awareness of their own addictive nature is really important.

You can only work on an addictive habit once you are aware of it, otherwise, you might just continue it subconsciously throughout life. Imagine, just one week out of your life can reveal so much about you! But the sad part is not many traders would be able to follow this even for just a week. They may end up quitting the detox after the second or third day.

The urge to check the prices may be so strong that they may feel that doing the detox was a bad idea and checking the prices will not harm as much. They may even think that they will check the prices just once and then continue the detox, but it does not work like that. Just checking the price once might send you down the slippery slope of checking prices multiple times again that day, and you will never be able to notice and observe your behaviours and patterns towards trading.

3. Have a clear plan

I know I have talked about it in this book, but it is so important that I will explain it in detail once again.

Most problems occur because you do not have a clear plan. It is not only true for trading but for life too. It is even said: "A fool with a clear plan is better than a genius without a plan."

Most traders out there just take random trades. They do not realise that they are just taking bets and not trades in that manner. They punch a trade and hope that it will work out in their favour. That is not a plan, it is just a gambler pulling the lever of a slot machine.

To make a clear plan, keep these pointers in mind:

i) **When exactly to enter:** Once you have done the scanning and shortlisted the trade, you should know the exact price to enter. Note it down in your notebook, journal, or just mark that point on the chart itself. You can simply put a horizontal line on the chart which will tell you that you need to buy that particular stock when the price crosses above that level. This might sound too simple, but it really works wonders. It will ensure that you enter according to plan and not out of FOMO or excitement.

ii) **How much to enter:** You need to also decide if you want to enter the full position once or you need to split it into parts, let us say, you want to enter 50% position when the breakout happens and 50% when the retest is done. This should also be planned before entering and not decided according to your emotions at the time of entering. Another thing you should be clear about is—do you take the position once or are you planning to pyramid (adding more positions along with the rise in price)? Pyramiding can be done in various ways—adding when the price breaks a new base or adding when the price comes to retest important moving averages like the 20-exponential moving average (EMA) or 50-EMA. Whatever the case may be, the plan should be made before entering the trade.

iii) **Stop-loss level:** This may be the most important factor. Always know where you need to cut your loss. This is literally the essence of risk management. If any trader fails to follow this, they will not stay in the game long enough. Once you know where you have to cut your loss, you literally remove the confusion and anxiety from the trading equation. By marking the stop-loss level before entering, you know exactly how much you are risking in a particular trade. Once you are ready to lose that amount if the trade does not go in your favour, you can trade without fear, focus on just the process of trading, and not be attached to the outcome. You can focus on just taking trades according to your setups and not according to the outcomes of each trade.

4. Cash is also a position

Trade only when you get a setup in your favour and the trend is intact. Do not trade just because you have funds available and are sitting idle in front of the trading terminal.

Legendary trader Mark Minervini also mentions that he is in 50% cash at least 50% of the time, which means that if he feels that the market is not giving any opportunity to trade, then he just sits and waits. He does not have the urge to trade every time. In fact, he also suggests that there is a hard penny and easy penny environment which simply means that the trend is sometimes so strong that it is relatively easy to make money in the markets, and sometimes the markets might be so choppy and sideways that there will not be any clear trend and traders end up getting chopped on both sides. They might buy a stock and soon after, their stop-loss might get hit. Or, if they short a stock (selling a stock and then covering it later), again, their stop-loss might get hit. No matter what they do, the market would be ready to take their stop-loss. It usually happens when the trend is not clear and there is a lot of confusion in the market scenario.

During such times, it is wise to stay in cash and wait for better trending markets. A bird would also sit down on a tree's branch or on the ground for some time if the conditions are too windy and not in its favour, and fly again only when the conditions are a bit better. But as traders, you have this urge to constantly take action which makes traders lose money most of the time. Your goal should be to do quality trades and not worry about the quantity of trades. You usually trade much better when you are very selective about your trades and are willing to reject most of them, only selecting the ones which look perfect according to your strategy or analysis.

STOP

10

STOP DOING THESE TO BECOME A PROFITABLE TRADER

IF YOU MAKE
A PROFIT, BE
GRATEFUL FOR THE
MONEY.

IF YOU MAKE
A LOSS, BE
GRATEFUL FOR THE
LESSON.

If you want to be successful, you need to focus on all the things you need to reach that goal. But you also need to pay attention to the things which you should definitely not do! It is usually the big mistakes that make all the difference. Avoid these pitfalls and you can ensure a smoother trading experience.

1. Shifting strategies

Most traders keep looking for that perfect strategy which will solve all their trading problems and they would not have to learn anything else after that. But there is no such thing as a perfect strategy. The book *Stock Market Wizards* by Jack D. Schwager talks about many legendary traders.

Almost all of them have different strategies and are really successful in their respective trading and investing careers. This illustrates that we can have different styles and strategies and can make a decent amount of money, we do not have to keep trying to find that perfect strategy. Whenever a new trader enters the markets, the first few years of their learning curve are spent looking for that perfect strategy. They realise much later that they have been running in the wrong direction. Most legendary traders have very basic strategies and their charts are really clean (they follow only price action or just a few basic indicators if at all).

Strategy is just 20% of the total trading equation. What matters most is your:

- psychology,
- mindset,
- reaction towards the markets, and
- risk management.

You will trade much better if you focus more on these aspects instead of chasing strategies. Some trader might easily manage a small loss whereas another may start panicking at the sign of even the smallest loss. On the other hand, a trader may easily ride a wave of profit for much longer and try to capture the entire trend whereas another trader may feel the compulsion to book even the smallest amount of profit as they may fear that the profit may again turn into break even or even a loss.

I am not saying that you should not have any strategy. Your strategy is your GPS. It will tell you where to take a turn and when to stop. That is why you should try out a few strategies and observe which one suits you. Once you find that strategy, stick to it religiously and do not keep hopping to every other strategy you get to know about after that.

2. Trying to earn a salary from markets

Sorry to disappoint you but trading is not a job where you can earn a certain amount every month. This is more like a business where you earn in seasons—not monthly, weekly or daily. Many new traders who enter the market keep asking me how much they can earn every month. The question itself is not correct. There may be many seasons where you may earn handsomely and are able to make a profit which may be equal to the returns of 4–5 months in one month. And, there may be many months where you will not be able to make a single rupee. If you are not comfortable with not having stable earnings, then trading is not for you.

Trying to earn a certain amount every day may work for some time, but it usually does not end well. Many traders (including me) make this mistake and even start treating trading as their jobs. They reach office on time (they are ready to trade the markets as soon as they open) and try to work hard by staying busy all day long. They think that this is how everything is done, assuming that they need to sit at the trading terminal all day long and keep trading day in and day out. They assume that the greater the number of trades that they take, the better their chance of getting a profit.

But the opposite is always true. Trading is not a job. Stop treating it like one.

You do not need constant action to make money in the markets. You need to act only when the setup or trend is in your favour and simply sit on your hands when the trend is missing. As pioneer trader Jesse Livermore rightly said, "Money is made by sitting, not trading."

Another issue you face when you start treating trading as a job is that you try to earn something constantly from the markets. You may be under the impression that you will be able to extract a fixed amount of revenue from the markets on a monthly basis, just like a salary. But this is not how the markets work. Nothing like this exists in the markets. In fact, the more you try to earn something all the time from the markets, the more you would trade unnecessarily without any proper setup and make losses. The more you try to recover those losses, the more losses you would face as you would be trading out of fear and not based on your analysis and logic. That would result in even more losses and the vicious circle would keep on repeating itself. Once a trader gets stuck in this kind of a situation, it is really hard to escape from it. It usually does not end well. The only solution is to not get into this kind of a situation in the first place.

If you really need to make money from trading

like your life depends on it, it is unlikely that you would ever make it, and even lose your own savings. Never trade with the money you cannot afford to lose because you would lose it eventually if you trade with your emotions, rather than a fixed setup. This is the reason I urge everyone to not quit their job to pursue trading full time. It is always better to have a job or business from which you earn your main source of income which would take that earning pressure off your head. You would be able to take rational decisions and your trading experience would be seamless and efficient.

3. Avoid catching tops and bottoms

Trying to catch tops and bottoms is a fool's errand. There is literally no benefit in catching the tops and bottoms if you cannot ride the trend after that any longer. Buying a stock at the exact bottom might look good on paper, and yes, you may be able to show off to your friends. But if you cannot ride the trend after entering, what is the point? It is said that it is always better to be a bit late for a good party than to be very early for a bad one. This basically means that you should enter a trade only once the trend has been established, which usually means that you would enter the trade a bit late. But that is okay. Do not worry about the 2–3% that you left on the table by not buying the stock at the exact bottom because you are more focused on the next 50–70% or even 100% of the move that you are going to ride after entering, as long as the trend is intact. You must have heard stories of legendary traders who made huge amounts of money from the markets. None of them made it by catching the tops and bottoms and almost every one of them made serious amounts of money by riding the trends for longer.

Do not obsess over catching the exact top or bottom of a move. Instead, focus on identifying and riding the trend that follows. That is where the real money is made in trading.

When anyone enters the market, they usually try to hunt the exact tops and bottoms of every move as it gives a sense of accomplishment and a dopamine hit. They feel very excited that they were able to catch the exact top or bottom of a move. They jump around telling their friends that as soon as they entered, the stock made the low on the exact same day. But traders who have a bit of experience and have spent some time in the markets realise that it literally does not matter much to nail the exact entry point if we do not have the capacity to hold the trade after entering. In easy terms, you do not have to capture the entire move of a trade from 0 to 100. You can enter at 15 and exit at 80 and still make huge profits.

How can you ride the trend for longer? By using trailing stop-loss. In the trailing stop-loss method, you exit the position by trailing the profits. You keep moving the stop-loss levels up as the price moves upwards. You can do this by manually moving up the stop-loss level by marking the stop-loss level on the chart according to the basic price action.

Or, you can use indicators like moving averages or super trend. These indicators make it really easy to trail the stop-loss without much effort. The indicator itself will tell you when to book out profits. Yes, you will not be able to exit at 100, as mentioned earlier. You will be able to exit at 80 once the price moves up to 100 and then retraces towards 80. There is no way to exit at the exact top and there is no need to do that either. In trading, capture a major chunk of the move and shift your capital to the next available trade. No one can capture the bottom and top of every move and it is not needed either. So do not fret over it and focus more on psychology and risk management. They play a much bigger role in trading profitably.

New traders who put too much emphasis on the entry, enter at 0 or maybe 2, but exit at 10 and regret when they see the stock continue its move towards 100.

4. Stop following most online influencers

This was a great step that helped my trading immensely. There are too many influencers out there who show off their profits on a daily basis. I had started following a few of them and whenever they posted a big profit, I would get intimidated and start trading in big quantities to match those numbers. They made me believe that making these kinds of profits on a daily basis was normal. I doubted my strategy, my learning about the markets and my self-confidence whenever I was unable to make profits. The influencers would show off their lifestyle too. They flaunted their luxury cars and huge offices. I was not learning anything from them, just getting envious and jealous of them. It made me wonder, if both of us know the same technical analysis, how come these guys are making so much profit and I am not?

It was much later that I realised that most of these traders or influencers were actually faking their lifestyles and their profit screenshots as well! They were doing all that to sell their services. There is nothing wrong in selling a service if you have the experience and knowledge about a field. But do not fake something just to sell your services. I would urge everyone to not follow anyone online if you do not get any real value from them.

TRADING JOURNAL				
DATE	NAME	QTY	P/L	REASON ENTRY EXIT

11

TRADING JOURNAL

MOST TRADERS WANT 10X RETURNS BUT DO NOT WANT TO JOURNAL 10 MINUTES A DAY.

SUCCESS IS NOT MAGIC. IT IS THE BORING STUFF DONE CONSISTENTLY.

A trading journal is nothing but a log that traders can use to record their trades. Therefore, it is one of the most effective tools to improve the trading skills of a trader.

A good trading journal serves two purposes:
1) It helps to *track the progress* of trading, and
2) It also *highlights the mistakes* committed by a trader.

There are many benefits of a trading journal. Some of them are listed below:

1. *It helps to identify the weakness of a trader*. After identifying it, if a trader avoids such failed trades, he will immediately fall into the breakeven zone (no loss, no profit).

2. *It helps to fine-tune the trading strategy.* You can modify your trading strategy based on the results you get.
3. *It helps to identify the conditions under which a trader is getting success.* Later, a trader can take a little more risk to maximise the profits.
4. *A trading journal can tell you everything about a trader.* In simple words, it is like the mark sheet of a student.

How to create a trading journal

Creating a trading journal is easy, and traders should include all the details related to their trading.

Step 1: Pick a source to log the information. It can be your own spreadsheet or online journal. I suggest picking your own trading spreadsheet.

Step 2: Identify all the information which needs to be recorded in the journal. Some of the mandatory details are instrument name, entry date, entry reason, entry price, exit date, exit price, exit reason, stop-loss, learnings, etc.

Trade #	Instrument Name	Entry Date	Entry Price	Quantity	Entry Reason	Stop-loss	% Risk in Portfolio	Exit Date	Exit Price	Exit Reason	Success/Failure	Risk-Reward	Mistakes/Learnings
1	Tata Motors	26-03-2021	295	100	Trading System-1	281	2%	8/4/2021	313	Trail SL hit	Success	1-1.3	Execution error
2	Reliance	30-03-2021	2015	25	Trading System-2	1970	1.50%	5/4/2021	1970	SL Hit	Failure	N/A	Selling is strong

Step 3: When the template is ready, log all your trades in it. Never postpone this step.

Step 4: Once you have sufficient data (25–100 trades), compile the data and study where you are making mistakes. Then, try to avoid these mistakes going forward.

Traders can use the trading template (see previous page) to log their trades.

Importance of a Trading Journal

With a good trading journal, traders can fine-tune their trading strategy or system over time. It also helps to cut down the emotions while managing trades (either entry or exit).

Successful traders rely on a profitable trading framework. A good trading journal is a valuable input for the trading framework and helps traders manage their trades in different market conditions.

Trading psychology plays a crucial role in trading success. Many traders experience different kinds of emotions that lead to unplanned trading activities in the live market. Maintaining a trading journal allows you to record your emotions during the live market, identifying the source of such feelings later. This awareness and self-assessment accelerates your success in trading.

Documentation of every trade makes you accountable for every action. As you know, successful trading is all about making better trading decisions. Taking accountability for every move is the first step towards making better decisions in the future. It helps linear growth. A trader cannot execute the same quantity every time he aims to achieve good growth in this field.

THE MARKET IS NOT CLOSED FOR SERIOUS TRADERS ON WEEKENDS.

THIS IS THE TIME TO SHARPEN YOUR SWORD BY:

- READING BOOKS
- WATCHING INTERVIEWS/ DOCUMENTARIES
- SCANNING STOCKS FOR NEXT WEEK

2 INTERVIEWS

01

STEVE BURNS

TENNESSEE, USA

1. Please tell us briefly about your educational background. When did you first hear about the markets?

While my traditional academic education ended with my high school diploma, my self-education continued with reading over 1,000 non-fiction books and over 400 of those were in the investing, trading, and finance category. At one time I was rated the most helpful trading book reviewer on Amazon, approximately 13 years ago. My love for reading and self-education continues to this day as I average reading one book per week.

I started looking at compound capital growth charts in the late 1980's as a teenager. Around the same time, I started looking at stock quotes in the newspaper and watched how they moved daily. I have always loved capitalism and business operations, so the stock market was a natural extension of this interest. My plan at the age of 19 was to use the stock market to grow a large sum of capital and become financially independent.

2. What were the problems you faced in your initial trading months/years?

I was lucky as my first attempt of simply investing in high growth and tech mutual funds in the 1990's worked from the start. Investing seemed very easy and I was off to compounding and growing my capital year over year and sometimes daily.

My first real education came in the year 2000 as the market peaked and I learned how fast a sector can go down. I spent 2001 and 2002 getting a better game plan together to come out of my drawdown and get to my equity peak and start growing my capital again. This started my real journey as a trend trader and learning how to cut losses and lock-in big gains while they were still there.

3. Which markets do you trade and what is your trading style?

I am a swing trader who trades big cap growth

stocks, exchange traded funds, IPOs, and options at times. I will trade longer term trends when there is no good reason to exit a big winning swing trade.

4. Did you incur losses when you started trading? How did you overcome that difficult time and stay motivated?

I did not incur any long term losses from 1992 until the dotcom meltdown in March of 2000 when I could no longer get back to new all-time highs in capital. I was more of a long term investor and focused on holding and rotating my portfolio to be as aggressive as possible.

Of course I had drawdowns on each market pull back, but they did not last long as the NASDAQ would eventually make a new all-time high and my capital along with it, in most instances. Back then I thought stocks only went up. I learned a lot from my first big –50% drawdown in capital from March 2000 to early 2003. I got back to my peak around 2005.

5. How do you presently trade? (Please give examples along with charts if possible.)

My favourite swing trading signals now are

5-day/20-day EMA crossover signals on daily charts and I ride winners until they have bearish candlestick reversals or become overbought near the 70 RSI. Here is one of the trade examples I am currently still in right now $QQQ. (See chart)

6. What is your advice to new traders?

If you want to be a trader, the first step is to create a quantified trading system with a positive expectancy. Then trade it with proper diversification, position sizing, and discipline over the long term. Do not be a gambler or trade like in a casino.

7. Which books do you suggest everyone should read?

For new traders I suggest starting with my book *New Trader, Rich Trader* and then advancing through my other books. For more experienced traders, some of the best trading books ever written are *The Market Wizards* series by Jack Schwager and *Trend Following* by Michael Covel, if you want to understand how the best professional traders and money managers really trade.

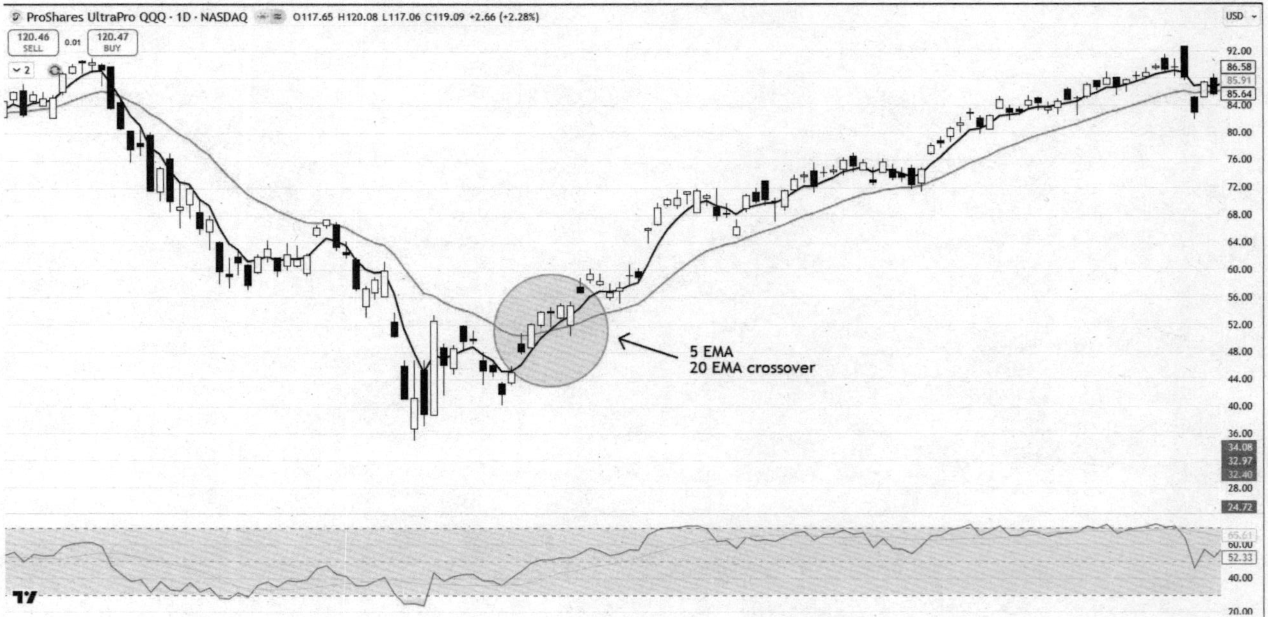

Daily chart of Ultrapro QQQ (TrendSpider chart).

02

INDRAZITH SHANTHARAJ

BENGALURU, INDIA

1. Please briefly tell us about your educational background. When did you first hear about the markets?

Thanks for the opportunity.

I have an Engineering Degree (IT), and like a typical Bangalorean, I started my career in the software industry.

I joined Australia and New Zealand Banking Group (ANZ) in 2007. Most of my colleagues played with markets, and I started buying and selling some shares along with them.

But I have another story that inspired me to take a serious look at the markets. It is a big story, and I have explained this story in my book, *Price-Action Trading*.

The short story is I have a close friend who is super-intelligent and got success in all areas of life except the stock market. He lost all his savings (in fact, more than his savings) when Nifty hit the upper circuit in May 2009.

From that day on, I became inquisitive about the markets.

2. What were the problems you faced in your initial trading months/years?

Since the beginning, I had a particular liking for intraday trading. It is not only because of quick money, but there is also no need to worry about overnight risk—the next day will be a brand new day.

During those days, brokerage for day trading was too high. I still remember, one day I was able to catch some points profit in Nifty, and I was happy. But when I looked at the statement at EOD, it was negative because I had to pay some extra money due to high brokerage.

All these problems disappeared when Zerodha was introduced.

Besides, managing trading along with my job was really challenging.

3. Which markets do you trade, and what is your trading style?

I trade only in Indian markets.

I trade only Nifty and BankNifty for intraday trading.

For positional trading, I observe all the good stocks in Nifty.

I use market profile concepts for my intraday trading and breakout/price-action trading for my positional bets.

Depending on the market conditions, I use different trading instruments in intraday trading.

For example, before the introduction of weekly options, I was a pure options buyer at the intraday level.

After the availability of weekly options, volume reduced in monthly options, and time decay (theta) was working against me in weekly options. Hence, during that time, I shifted to futures trading.

Once Covid-19 started, both the Nifty and Bank Nifty daily range increased a lot. Earlier a 500–600 points move in a day in Bank Nifty was a rare scenario. In 2020–2021, Bank Nifty was giving that move almost every day.

So in the futures, my position size reduces automatically (to maintain the same risk); hence the profit will also be less.

Due to this change, I shifted to the options selling game. Most of the time, I deploy a credit spread strategy. Sometimes, I do use the Iron Condor strategy and options buying.

4. Did you incur losses when you started trading? How did you overcome that difficult time and stay motivated?

I have committed most of the blunders in trading.

Whenever I lost big money, I would take a break for a few days and come back, try again.

I thought there is a magic indicator, and it was the secret to make lots of money in trading. I had attended many trading seminars during that time.

But later, I realised that money management and trading psychology play a significant role in trading. Everyone commits mistakes, and I was no different. I would take more risk per trade, and whenever I faced some failures, I would feel bad for two reasons: 1) the pain of losing money and 2) the difficulty in accepting the failure.

Later I reduced my risk to 2% per trade, and then the first problem (pain of losing money) dissolved automatically (as I was not losing a big chunk of my portfolio).

Meditation helps me to accept failure and move on in my trading.

There is no better teacher than the market itself. Whenever I felt I knew everything and could make more money, I would get a bigger loss on the following day itself. So, I have decided to be humble, maintain a learning mindset forever instead of losing money to the market!

5. How do you presently trade? (Please give examples along with charts if possible.)

Positional Trade

I use simple price action and breakout trading concepts for my positional trades.

The holding period varies between 2 days to 1 month, and I share most of my positional trades on Twitter to educate people.

I am very crazy about breakout trades as they bring a good move in quick time (means in one day).

I look for the below indicators to opt for a breakout trade:

1) A big breakout candle
2) The breakout should come in quick time
3) Absence of selling in the breakout candle
4) Good volume on the breakout candle

Image 1 shows a good breakout trade opportunity in Mindtree on 10th March 2021.

It satisfied all the requirements (4 parameters), hence I took a long trade above the breakout candle on the next trading day.

After making the entry, I prefer to trail stop-loss below the swing lows or in case of a big bearish candle, below the low of that candle.

In image 2, the points labelled 1, 2,3, and 4 are my trail stop-loss points. It hit my stop-loss on 13th April.

Intraday Trade

I refer to the last few days' trading activities and the previous day's market sentiment for my intraday trades.

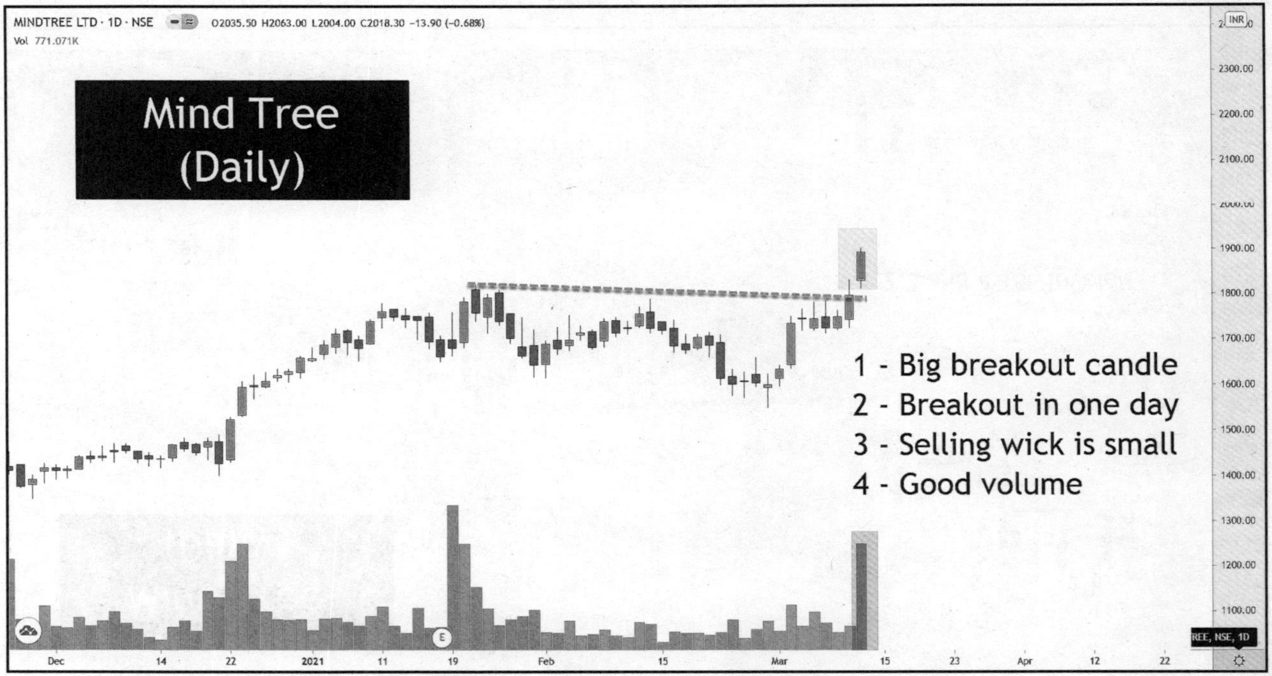

Image 1: Mindtree breakout trade on 10 March 2021

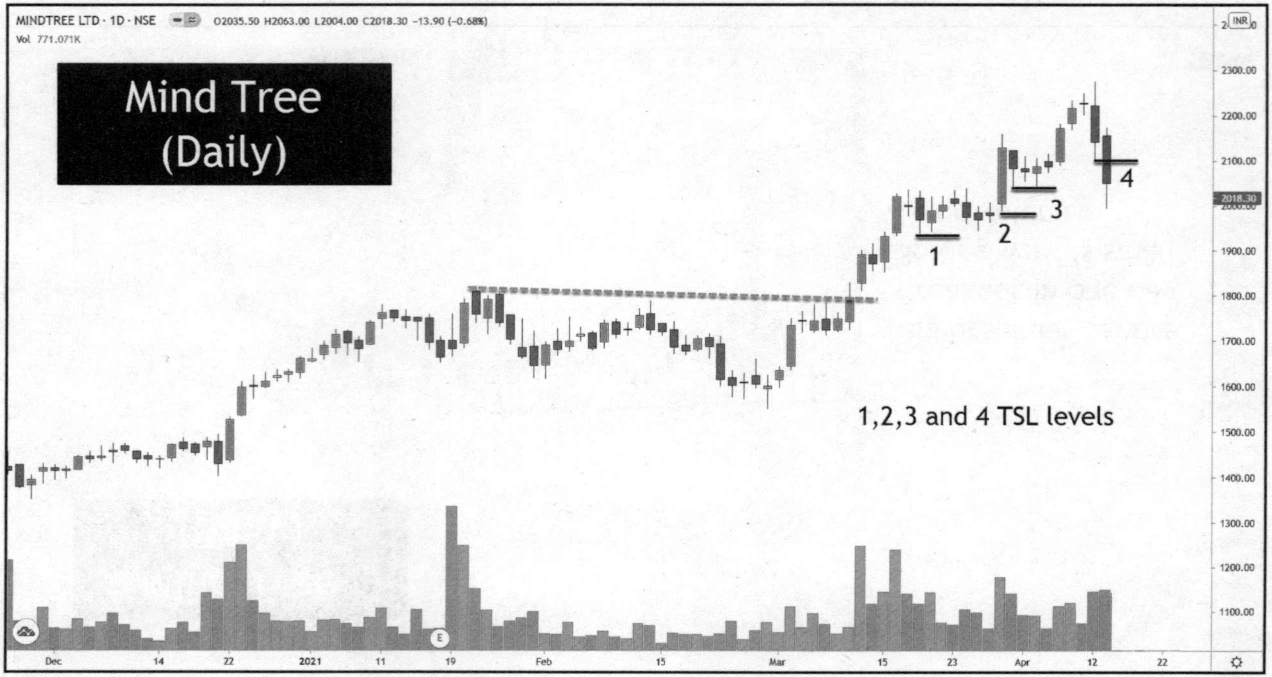

Image 2: Mindtree breakout trade result

If we look at the Nifty daily chart in image 3, one thing is clear: sellers are dominating in the last 1–1.5 months.

The previous day's market sentiment is negative as it opened with a big gap and closed at a day's low.

Coincidently the day's low aligns with the previous swing low (just 19 points difference).

So, there is a possibility of a big move if it breaks the 14260 levels (highlighted), and I plan to take short trade for the next day (I will maintain this view unless I see a clear rejection of price at 14260).

But taking a proper entry is essential.

In my opinion, only 'entry' and 'exit' decide the fate of our trade, and everything else is useless.

I did not opt for any open action trade as the price did not break the 14260 (previous swing low) or 14280 (previous day low).

At 9.30 a.m. (after 15-minutes of the market opening), it was clear that there are some buyers during the open action, and they do not want the price to trade below the previous day (image 4).

So, my next option was to wait until the buying got exhausted or selling became evident.

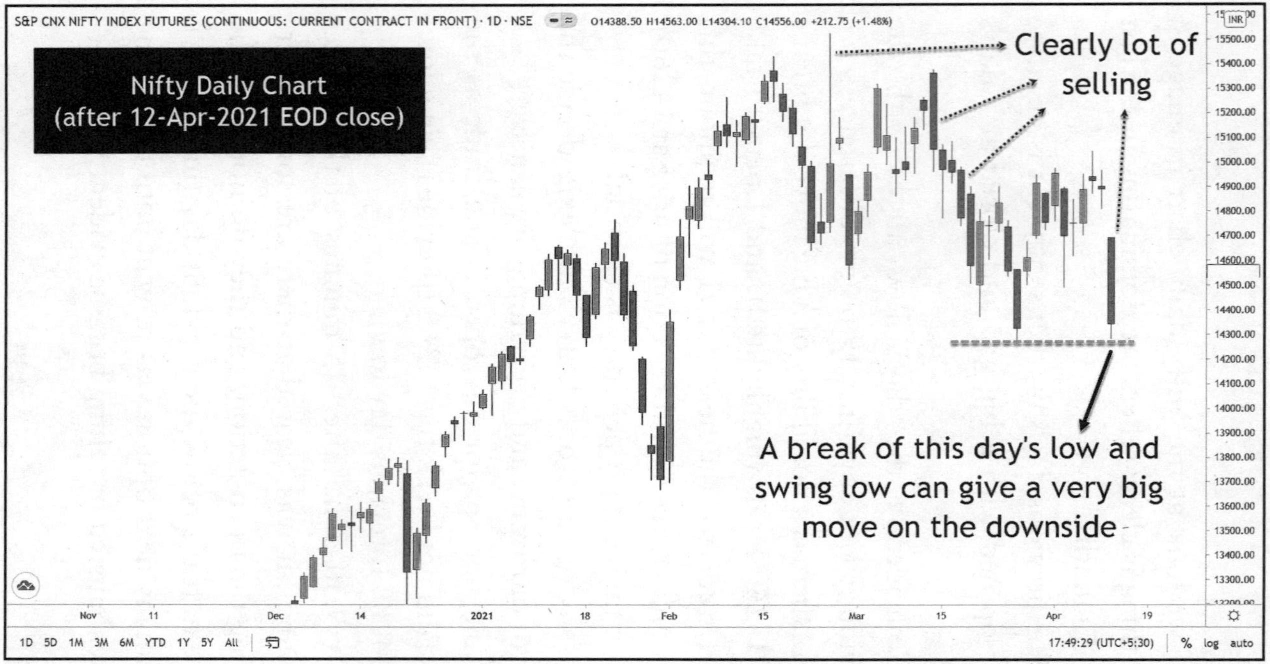

Image 3: Daily chart of Nifty after the market closed on 12 April 2021

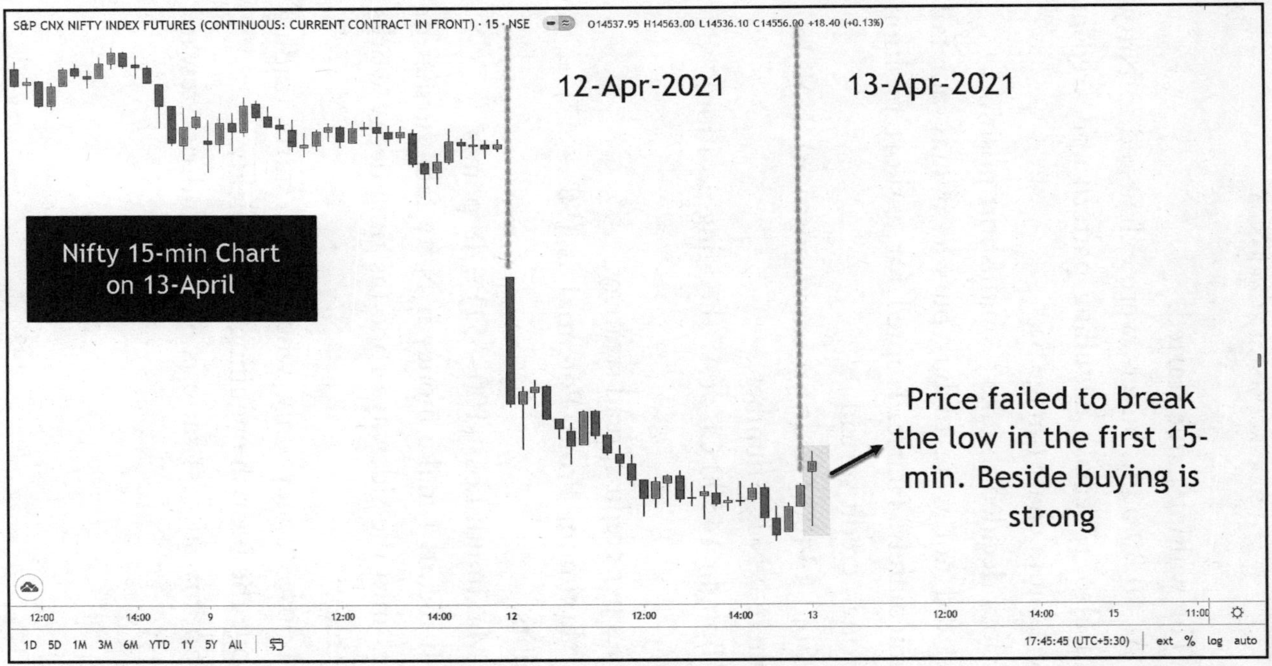

Image 4: 15-min chart of Nifty at 9.30 a.m. on 13 April 2021

The waiting game started.

At 10.30 a.m., buyers were exhausted in Nifty, and also, a bearish engulfing pattern appeared in the 15-min chart (image 5).

So, I decided to take a small short position.

I did not want to buy puts as it may not fall immediately. Hence, I opted for a short position through credit spread.

Sold 14400 CE at 98 (main position) 'NN' lots (where NN is a number)

Bought 14500 CE at 47 (hedging position) 'NN' lots.

As per credit spread strategy,

Maximum Profit Potential is (98 – 47) = 51 points.

Maximum Loss (100 – 51) = 49 points.

It means I make money if Nifty falls further or goes into the sideways zone (as time decay works for me).

I lose money only when Nifty starts trading above the bearish engulfing level quickly.

So, my success ratio is 66.6%, and risk-reward is 1:1.

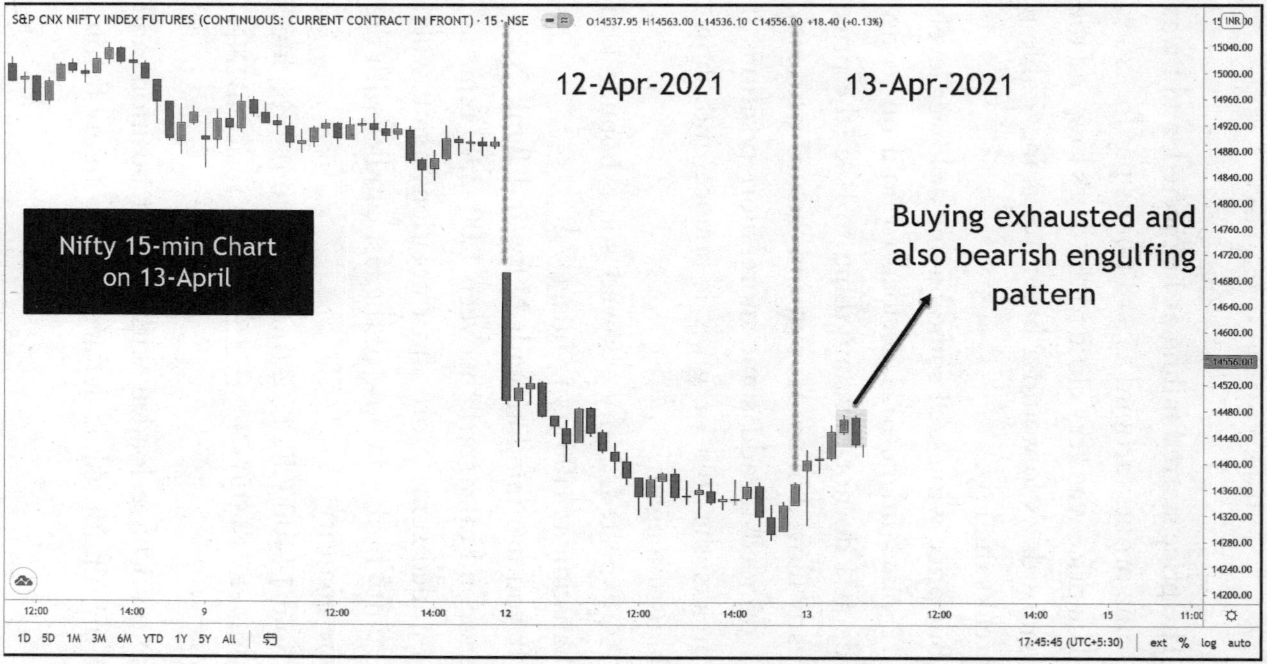

Image 5: 15-min chart of Nifty at 10.30 a.m. on 13 April 2021

The price started falling as I expected, and I was in some profits (around 17–18 points per lot).

The price was very close to the day's low and the previous day's low, and a big move is inevitable if it breaks the low.

But price witnessed some buying at lower levels at 12 p.m. (image 6). I decided to hold on to my trade as I do not have anything to lose (the price already moved in my favour, and theta is with me).

I decided to add some more short positions if it breaks the low or gives a bounce and shows exhaustion again.

As expected, Nifty showed some bounce and exhaustion at 1:00 p.m. (image 7).

If you are familiar with Nifty and Bank Nifty, the second rally starts between 1:00–2:00 p.m.

I added some more short positions again when the Nifty broke the low of the last candle (with the same quantity).

Sold 14400 CE at 72 (main position) 'NN' lots

Bought 14500 CE at 31 (hedging position) 'NN' lots.

Now I have loaded with a short position, and the maximum risk is defined, theta is in my favour.

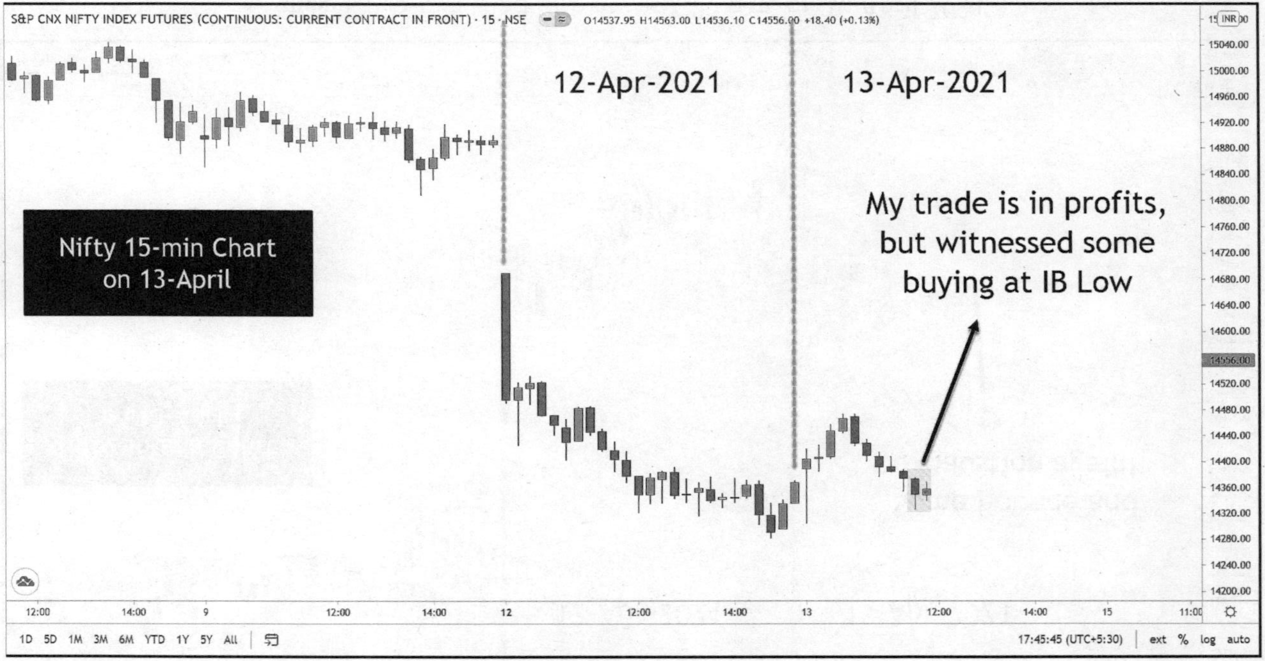

Image 6: 15-min chart of Nifty at 12.00 p.m. on 13 April 2021

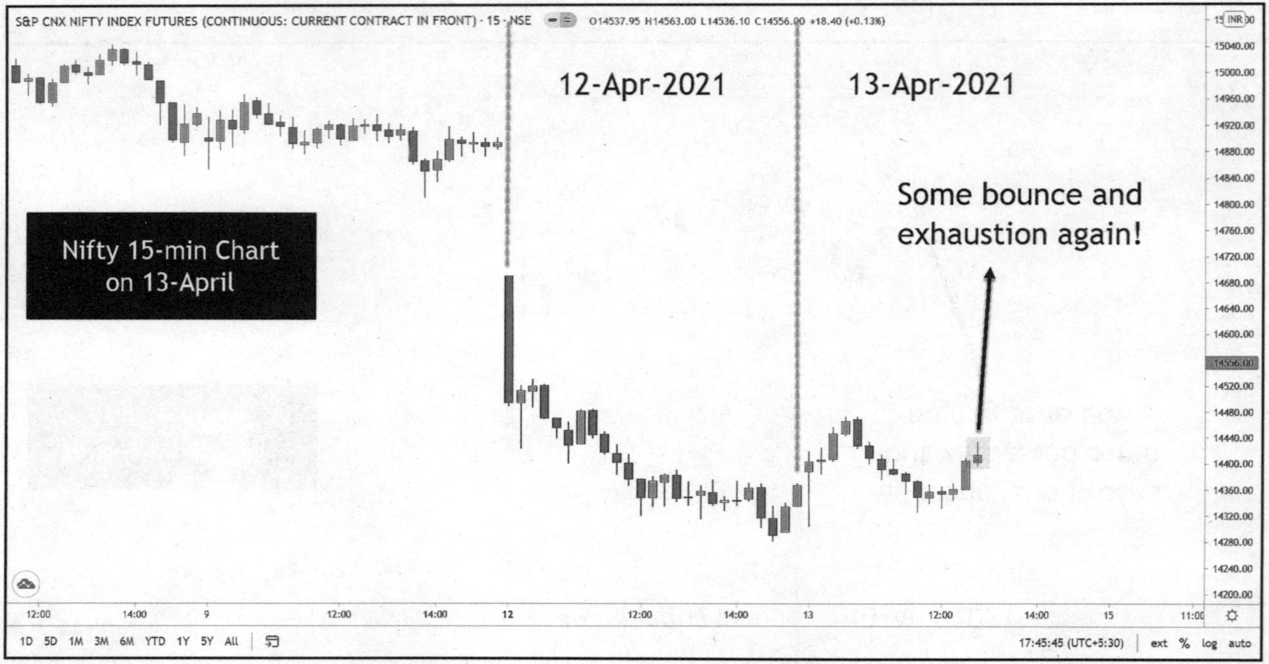

Image 7: 15-min chart of Nifty at 1.00 p.m. on 13 April 2021

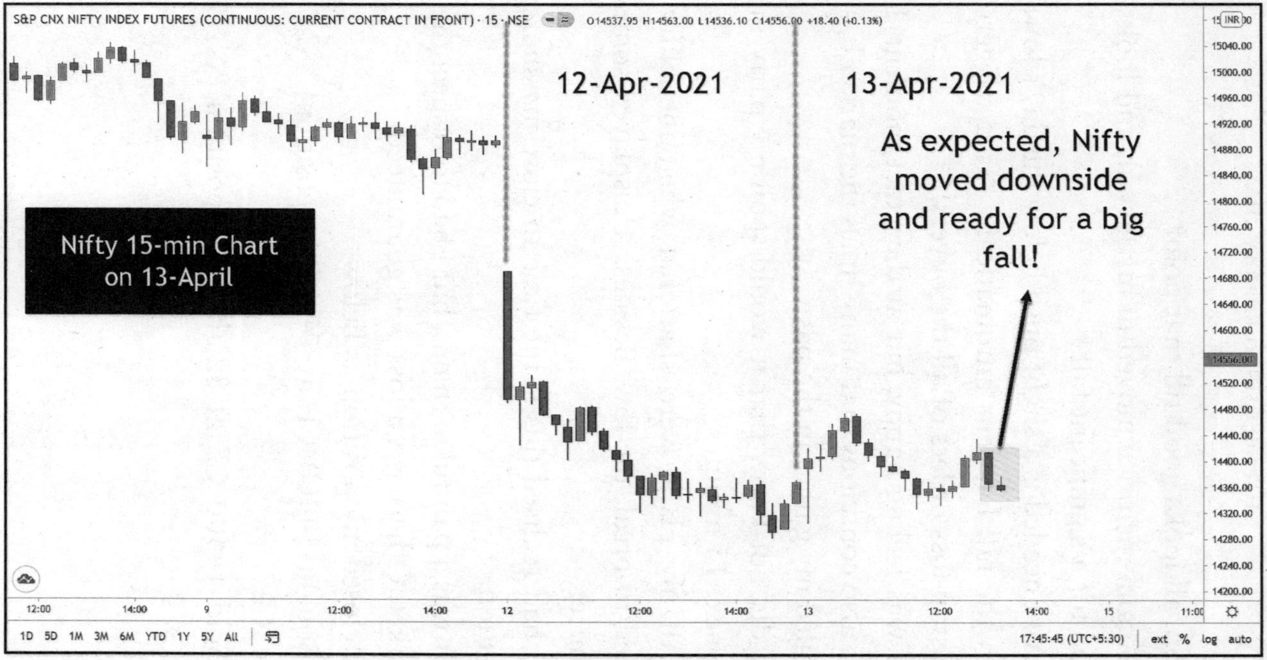

Image 8: 15-min chart of Nifty at 1.30 p.m. on 13 April 2021

So, all looks good till that point.

Again, the price moved in my favour, and looks good for a significant fall.

All I needed is a slight push below the day's low, then the fall happens automatically (as it triggers the stop-loss orders of all the buyers).

I was feeling happy, but at the exact moment, I was also conscious that many times the market has spoiled my games in the past.

I did not know that it would spoil my party in the next 15 minutes.

All my plans were shattered when the Nifty failed to break the low. Besides, it displayed some bounce.

I had realised this is the time to close my short position.

It was a painful moment, but I had to respect the market. Otherwise, a loss was guaranteed.

I closed my position as below:

Bought 14400 CE at 74 (main position) 'NN' lots X 2

Sold 14500 CE at 32 (hedging position) 'NN' lots X 2

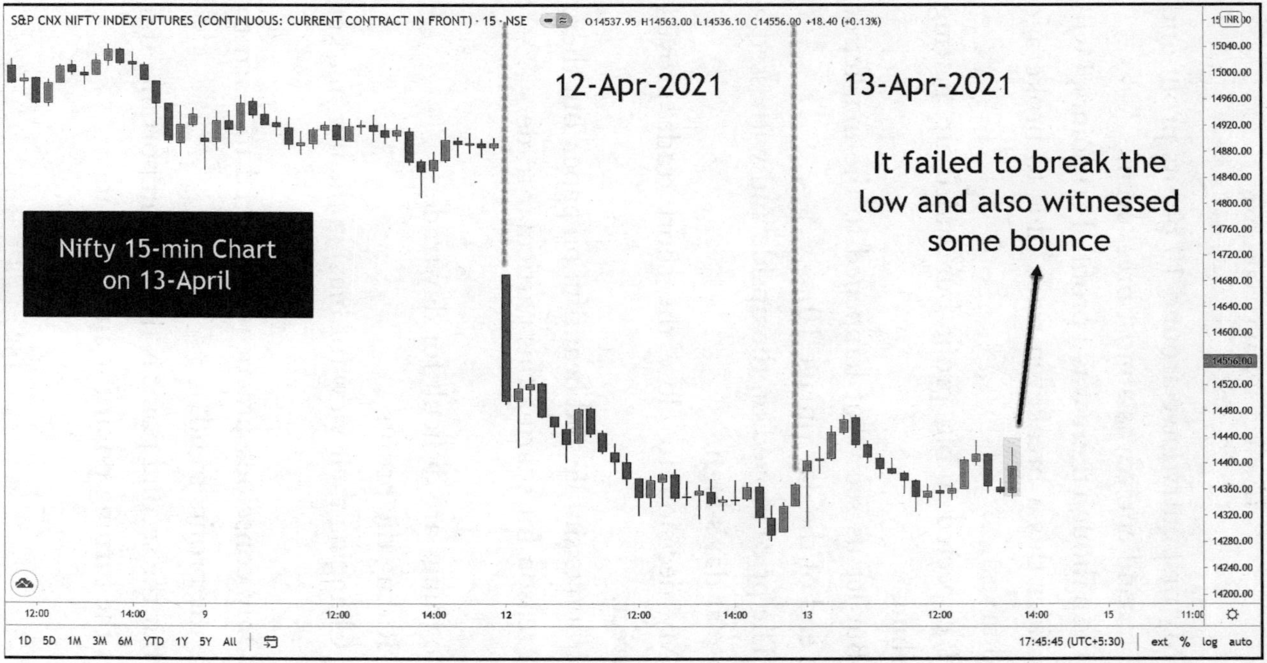

Image 9: 15-min chart of Nifty at 1.45 p.m. on 13 April 2021

My first entry gave around 10 points profit and the second entry was almost breakeven.

Even though there was a profit of 10 points, I will consider this a breakeven trade (due to brokerage and taxes).

I expected a big profit but ended up getting nothing.

But let us see what happened to the market at the end of the day (image 10).

The price moved on the upside and witnessed a close at day's high.

My decision to close the short trade proved correct.

It looks simple and beautiful on paper. But there is a reason for sharing this particular trade.

Two things are difficult for day traders:

1. Riding the profits
2. Changing their view (or bias) in the live market

Only conscious practice is required to learn to ride the profits trend.

But the second point is the most important, and it is the turning point for any day trader.

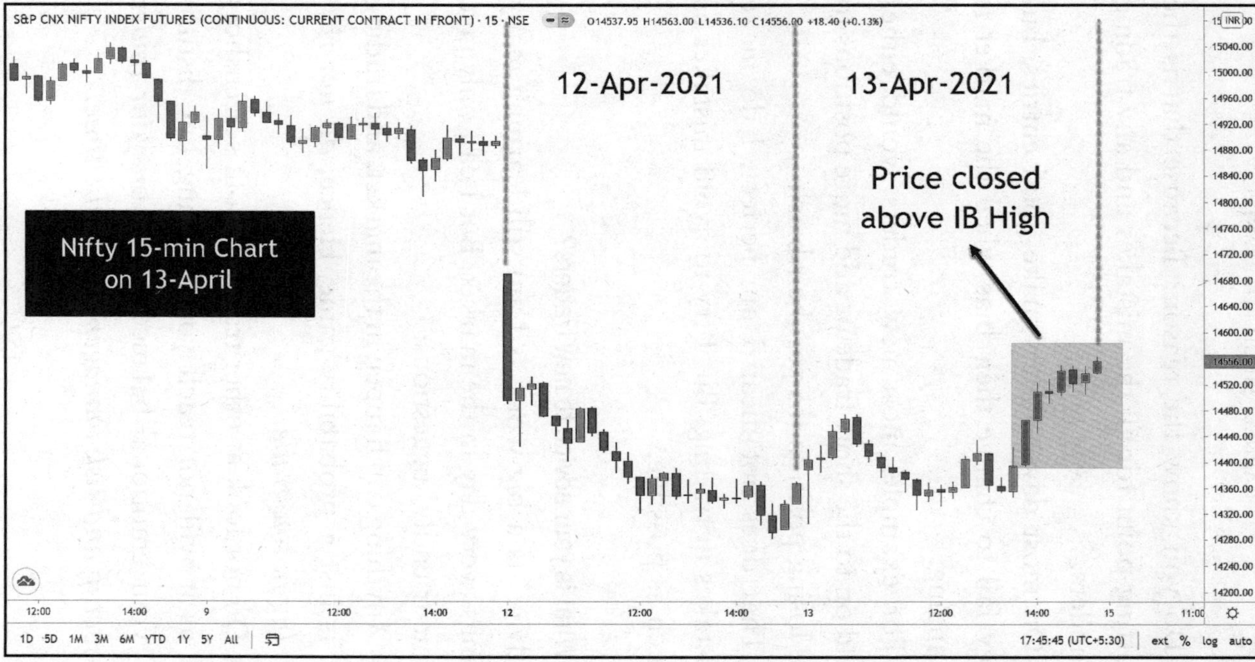

Image 10: 15-min chart of Nifty at the end of the day on 13 April 2021

Do you know the reason? Because that is the starting point for all the mistakes and any trading blunders.

On most days, traders make good entries, but they fail to change their bias when the market is changing.

For example, most new traders would either hold on to the short trade or add more positions to the losing position (as per their bias).

That does not mean I am perfect. I do make mistakes in trading. But I try to avoid mistakes as much as possible.

6. What is your advice to new traders?

'Advice' is a big word as I am still learning many things every day in the market. But I can only give some friendly suggestions:

- Anything can happen in the market, and trading is just a probability game. Hence, *do not risk big in one trade*.
- Do not look at other traders' profit screenshots as it will not teach you anything but disturb your emotional balance. *Focus on your trader setup and risk management all the time.*

- Whenever you get into a lower timeframe, you find more opportunities, but risk and noise also increases. So *pick a timeframe that suits your mindset and time availability*.
- Any debate over a trading concept is not necessary. *If you are making money, you are right; otherwise, you are wrong.*
- *'Trading psychology' and 'risk management' are equally important* as compared to technical analysis. Please also focus on these two aspects.
- Trading is a small aspect of life. *Try to explore this beautiful life along with trading.* One can read books, travel to a different place, spend some time with nature, help needy people, learn some spiritual practices, etc.

7. Which books do you suggest everyone should read?

Being an author, I know the difficulty of writing a book. Articulating thoughts in words is a difficult task. Hence, I have immense respect for the below-mentioned books and their authors:

1) *Trading in the Zone* by Mark Douglas
2) *Trade Like a Casino* by Richard L. Weissman

3) *New Trader Rich Trader* by Steve Burns and Holly Burns
4) *How to Avoid Loss and Earn Consistently in the Stock Market* by Prasenjit Paul
5) *Master Mind of Day Trading* by Nataraj Malavade

Apart from these, people can also read articles on my blog:
https://www.profiletraders.in/blog

03

JAKE WUJASTYK

HIGHLANDS RANCH, CO, USA

1. Please briefly tell us about your educational background. When did you first hear about the markets?

I started trading at age 12 when my dad created a custodial trading account for me and wanted me to learn about the markets. I quickly became fascinated with the stock market and was fascinated with 'trends'. When I went to college, I studied economics which helped me understand the underlying forces moving price, supply and demand.

2. What were the problems you faced in your initial trading months/years?

My biggest issue trading initially was that I tried buying very small companies that had very low stock prices as I did not have a lot of money to use in the markets. This was something that did not work well at all, as most of these companies went to zero. I blew up my first trading account within 18 months.

3. Which markets do you trade and what is your trading style?

I generally trade the US equity markets and stocks that I am familiar with. I almost never trade a stock I have not been watching for weeks or months. It is important to understand the personality of the stocks you are trading to have an edge. I am a swing trader/position trader usually focusing on the daily and weekly charts.

4. Did you incur losses when you started trading? How did you overcome that difficult time and stay motivated?

Yes, I blew up my account rather quickly when I first started as I was trading very poor quality stocks and buying these because their stock price was low and I thought it was better to be able to buy 'a lot of shares'. The way I was able to stay motivated was by learning and reading as much as I could. Anytime I saw a term that I did not know, I would look it up and try to learn everything I could about it. A lot of education in trading is by going out and being a proactive learner.

5. How do you presently trade? (Please give examples along with charts if possible.)

I currently use Raindrop charts, anchored volume by price, simple chart patterns, and anchored VWAP to trade. These tools that I use on TrendSpider allow me to see supply and demand in a new light as well as see simple chart patterns setting up, using basic trendlines/zones. (Snowflake Inc. chart provided later).

6. What is your advice to new traders?

My advice to new traders is to focus on what works for you and your personality. One trading style may work great for one person and be a complete failure for another person. The only way to understand your personality in the markets is by experiencing wins and losses. Trading books are great to set a base knowledge, but experience teaches you about yourself and how you react to wins and losses.

Daily chart of Snowflake Inc.

7. Which books do you suggest everyone should read?

1. *Confessions of a Stock Market Addict* by Jim Cramer
2. *The Quants* by Scott Patterson

04

SOUMYA MALANI

KOLKATA, INDIA

1. Please tell us briefly about your educational background. When did you first hear about the markets?

I was one of the state toppers in secondary and higher secondary examinations. Coming from a business family, entrepreneurship and finance were the fields that always interested me. So I pursued my studies to become a chartered accountant (CA) and company secretary (CS), and I secured all-India ranks in both. However, I did not go on to finish those degrees since I got a dream opportunity to study at the London School of Economics, (LSE) where I completed an MSc in Accounting and Finance. The idea was always to gain as much knowledge as possible in the field of accounting and finance. The idea of accumulating degrees never motivated me. I was always motivated by a thirst for knowledge.

My grandfather would invest his savings in stock markets so right from childhood I was curious about the reds and greens flashing on the screen. When I was in primary school, annual reports would come in physical form. Even as a child, I would randomly glance through without understanding them even a bit. Neither did I know that these sometimes colourful and sometimes black and white books would become my partners for life.

2. What were the problems you faced in your initial trading months/years?

One of the most confusing things for a beginner in the market is that there are a million ways to trade or invest in the market and there are no right or wrong ways—it is all about your own mindset, strengths and weaknesses.

I firmly believe that in order to succeed in any field you need to have a clear-cut understanding of your strengths and weaknesses with respect to that field and then mould your style according to that.

When I came back from LSE, one thing was crystal clear to me that there would definitely be a massive difference between the theoretical and practical world. Hence, I wanted to shorten my practical learning curve by learning from those who have already excelled at what I had set my eyes on. In pursuit of the same, I travelled across the country and was fortunate to meet many of the topmost investors of India. The biggest lesson for me when I met them was that there is no single way to make money in the markets. All of these investors were super successful yet their styles were poles apart. This opened my mind and made me understand that the path which all of us try to find out is within us.

Once this realisation came about, I tried to read and gain more knowledge about the different ways in which the market can be approached because without that you would never be able to know which approach will suit you. I soon grasped the things that would match with my mindset and would give me returns as well as a good night's sleep when I followed them.

3. Which markets do you trade and what is your trading style?

I only trade in Indian stock markets. While

diversification across countries has its own benefits, personally I feel specialisation is very important. By focusing on one market, you gain a good understanding of the companies and their businesses over a period of time, which helps you to make smarter decisions.

I do both positional investing and swing trading. My entire approach towards stock picking is to find the strongest stocks. I am a strong believer in following the market rather than predicting it. I start by looking at charts of stocks and sectors that are hitting new highs. For any stock to be a multi-bagger it has to consistently hit new highs throughout its journey.

After that, I dig in deep to understand the fundamentals of the company, to understand the kind of growth that the company can post and for how long, as that is one of the most important factors that makes a company a multi-bagger.

As I spent more time in the markets and gained experience, I realised that multi-baggers have some common traits. Any stock that has the following lethal combination would have a massive potential to be a big multi-bagger:

Lethal Combination for a Multi-bagger

= Visionary Management
+ Scalability
+ Pricing Power
+ Tailwinds
+ High Growth
+ Higher Incremental return on capital employed (ROCE)
+ Low Equity
+ Under Ownership
+ Leader in a Niche Area

This approach helped me find life-changing multi-baggers such as Avanti Feeds, Bharat Rasayan, Apollo Tricoat, Minda Industries, Ajanta Pharma, Laurus Labs, etc. These stocks over a period of time have contributed massively to the growth of my portfolio.

Apart from that, I am also very active in start-up investing. It gives me the opportunity to interact with so many brilliant minds which helps me to cultivate my own ideas and to stay connected to ground realities.

4. Did you incur losses when you started trading? How did you overcome that difficult time and stay motivated?

Initially when I started trading, I would make the same mistakes that any newbie in the market makes—not cutting my losses fast, praying and waiting for my cost price to come, not riding my winners enough to make a meaningful difference to my trading account, and trying to buy the stocks that are falling in an attempt to buy them at the bottom.

Fortunately, I was quick to realise that the way I was approaching the market was like a hobby and not a profession. Hobbies are supposed to take money from you; whereas a profession is something that generates money for you. Hence, I made a 360-degree change in my approach towards the market.

I started to read about successful traders and investors and how they approached markets. I also spent hours and hours going back into history to understand the common factors that made a company a wealth creator or a wealth destroyer (I still do the same). I also worked a lot on understanding my strengths and mindset to work on strategies that would suit my personality.

I never really lacked motivation since it was crystal clear in my mind that I wanted to build a career in this field and there was no going back. I am fortunate to have a family that always supports me and believes in me. I think having a supportive family during your tough periods is the biggest blessing that one can have.

5. How do you presently trade? (Pease give examples along with charts if possible.)

I see myself as a "growth+momentum" investor. Regarding charts, my setup is very simple. I use price and volume along with 52-week high (which is denoted by the blue arrows). I try to look for strong price action in stocks that are hitting new highs. Once this is done I try and understand what the company does. After that, I use another filter criterion, which is a fundamental screener from where I try and understand how the company is performing in terms of its operations and whether the company fits my checklist.

Once a company satisfies these filter parameters, I then go on to do deep fundamental analysis on the company including scuttlebutt wherever possible before taking a final buy decision.

Note: The Scuttlebutt technique refers to a method of learning about a company and its investment merits by talking to many people in the company and industry, through which you can educate yourself thoroughly before making an investment.

Generally, people avoid buying stocks hitting a new high since the stock normally is up 50–100% by that time. However, one has to realise that there could be a big story unfolding and this could just be the start of something massive. The easiest way to discard a potential idea is to say, "It has already moved up a lot". Whereas the job of an investor is to try and understand why such a strong move has happened and whether it can still be a multi-bagger from these prices.

As you can see from the chart of Avanti Feeds that it was around Rs 13–14 when the stock made a new high after a long period in 2013. In that calendar year, the stock had a low of Rs 6.21 which means the stock was already up more than 100% from its lows when the stock came on my radar. However, the stock went on to hit a high of Rs 980 in less than 4 years. This was a life-changing investment for me where I made 70 times of my

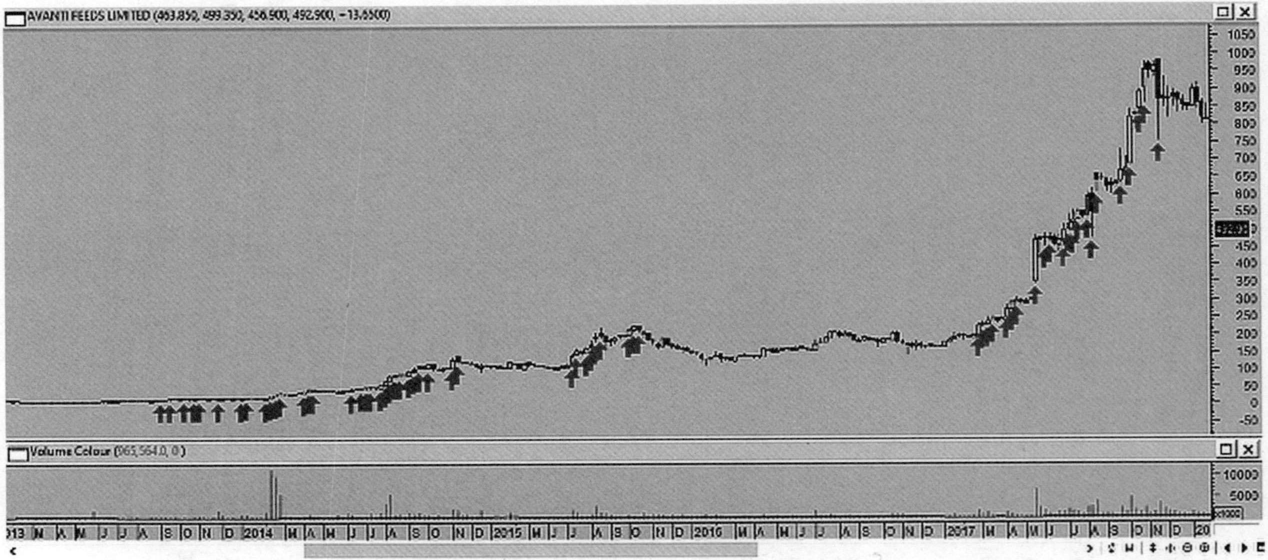

Weekly chart of Avanti Feeds (Metastock).

capital in 4 years with an allocation that reached 44% of my portfolio at one point in time.

The biggest mistake that I could have made when it hit a new high was to ignore the stock just by thinking it has already doubled in price. My mindset at that point was totally opposite—I was working doubly hard to figure out as much as I could about the business of the company and to understand what could be the potential thereon. While doing it I realised that there were massive tailwinds that were supporting the strong growth of the company backed by solid management which increased my conviction multi-fold.

The disclaimer here is that I am not suggesting that just because a company has hit a new high you go and buy it blindly. New highs are just a "starting point" or a filter, so that we can be with the strongest stocks in the market. Lots and lots of work is needed after that in order to shortlist the stock before buying it. Also, you must manage the risk and get out if the company is not performing as per your thesis.

6. What is your advice to new traders?

My advice to new traders would be to understand themselves and their personality in a better way and then trade accordingly. In markets, the tendency is to focus a lot on what is happening around us—however the answers that we are looking for lie within us. Be inspired by people, learn from them, but make your own path rather than blindly copying someone.

Also, your approach towards periods of losses and drawdowns determines how strongly you come back again. Losses are like tuition fees that every trader has to give to the market to learn the art. However, the most important thing is to learn from the losses. Mistakes cannot be avoided altogether but they can definitely be reduced if one takes full responsibility for his results and is making a conscious effort to improve.

7. Which books do you suggest everyone should read?

The following books have had a massive impact on my stock market journey and I would like to suggest the same for everyone to read:

- *One Up on Wall Street* by John Rothchild and Peter Lynch
- *Beating the Street* by Peter Lynch
- *How to Make Money in Stocks* by William J. O'Neil
- *Trade like a Stock Market Wizard* by Mark Minervini
- *Market Wizards* by Jack D. Schwager
- *Reminiscences of a Stock Operator* by Edwin Lefèvre
- *Think and Trade like a Champion* by Mark Minervini
- *Trading in the Zone* by Mark Douglas

05

JAMES GILLEN

NEW YORK, USA

1. Please briefly tell us about your educational background. When did you first hear about the markets?

The way I was first introduced to trading was through a friend who also happened to be my boss at that time. I can distinctly remember that he owned shares of Tesla stock which I believe were around $60.00 pre-split. His words were, "invest in Tesla and don't sell.". I wish I heeded his words, but I had my own notions about trading and hurdles I would need to overcome. I would have to learn the hard way which so many of us do.

If I had listened to him and invested in Tesla at that time, I would be a very rich man right now! He would always show me his portfolio and account of total gains. I was intrigued by the fact that you could buy shares of a company and compound your capital at such a high percentage the way that he was. This introduction to the investing world ignited a fire which would evolve into a career and passion that I did not plan. He was a buy and hold investor, and this was the trading style I wanted to emulate when I opened my first trading account.

2. What were the problems you faced in your initial trading months/years?

In the beginning of my trading career I lacked the discipline, knowledge, and patience and most importantly the 'seat time' needed to become a successful trader. I quickly shifted from wanting to be a long-term investor to a day trader. The quick action and massive gains were fascinating to me. I saw traders making hundreds to thousands of dollars in minutes and I wanted to do the same. I did not understand the fundamentals of trading which included risk management, position sizing, stop-losses and to never average down; simple things which are necessary to trade profitably.

These concepts were unknown to me and I paid for it early on. I would buy into one stock using my entire capital plus margin, I would win some and lose some. Eventually I took one giant loss which wiped out over 50% of my account. I felt depressed and discouraged that I lost so much money in such a short period of time. I cashed out my remaining capital from my trading account and hung up my hat for the next couple of years. I finally returned to the market during the short-lived 2020 COVID bear market, I saw an opportunity to capitalise on discounted stocks. Within weeks I had lost half my account again, a stock I sold for a loss I then watched run 50%–100% afterwards. I felt the same frustration and pain I did from my first major loss, but this time a fire ignited within me. A fire that set me on the course to learn, grow and evolve as a trader and to never take a large loss on my hard-earned money in the market again.

I read technical analysis books every night, studied patterns, candles, volume, moving averages, watched videos and read books on how to exercise proper risk management, position sizing and correct buy points. I studied charts every night and began to finally annotate my own charts.

This was a turning point in my trading career, when I turned inward to conquer trading rather than rely on what other traders were doing, which stocks they were buying. My inspiration was drawn from chartists like @TraderStewie @MadMraket @ TraderAmogh @PatternProfits @Patrickwalker56 and long-term investors such as @saxena_puru @ jonahlupton, position traders like @duckman1717 and @raytl—some of the great traders on Twitter.

I took a piece from all the traders I aspired to be like and turned it into my own style. I then turned that 50% loss into an 800% gain or 400% gain from my initial investment in less than a year. I thought I was a stock market wizard at this point, simply brilliant because I made 400% returns on my initial investment. Listen to me very closely, because I am about to give you some of the best advice out there, free of charge.

Making money is only half the battle when it comes to trading. The second half is keeping that money and locking in your gains! You are only as good as your last trade; locking in profit when the pickings are good is even more important than making those gains in the first place. The stock market will humble you, and it is usually after our biggest gains when we suffer our largest losses.

Protect your capital at all costs and always use a stop-loss. Risk management is always number one when it comes to my trading!

3. Which markets do you trade and what is your trading style?

I trade stocks that are on the NYSE which include common stocks, ETFs and recently I have started to trade crypto. I would describe my trading style as hybrid in nature; first and foremost a position trader, and second a swing trader.

My style is rooted in the teachings of William O'Neil which boils down to the strongest stocks from the strongest sectors with the best fundamentals. I am a breakout trader; I look for stocks in a consolidation period then position myself when that stock breaks out from a pattern (base). I have created a formula which I look for repeatedly in stocks, cryptos and ETFs.

I look for a specific pattern (bullish pennant, falling wedge, cup with handle), a volume shelf building around price within the pattern, and for the volume to dry up as price consolidates. I will then start a position when the stock breaks out from this pattern on HIGH volume. There are many factors which contribute to starting a new position, this is a basic breakdown, the bones of the trade, so to speak.

Once I am in a position that is working, I will ride the trend as long as possible, whether that is weeks, months, or years. I will trim profits on the way up and add to the position on pullbacks and new breakouts. I will completely exit the trade when there is a character change in the stock or when it breaks through a key moving average on high volume and it does not reclaim it immediately. This is a Cliff Notes version of my position trading strategy.

My swing trading is similar in the way I select the stocks that I position trade and at the buy point I enter the position. The only difference is that I hold the trade for a shorter duration of time, and I do not add to the trade. When I exit the swing trade, I will close out the entire position or I will sell half into strength and let the other half of shares ride. The trick is to consistently lock in profit, always lock in profit when it is available even if it is just a fraction of your position.

4. Did you incur losses when you started trading? How did you overcome that difficult time and stay motivated?

Early in my trading career I incurred heavy losses. As painful as the losses were—financially and mentally, it was the pain of those losses which gave me the fire and motivation to teach myself how to trade profitably. You must remember that trading is a journey and not a destination. Ironically the hardships, struggles, losses, and pain that come with learning the art of trading is the fuel which forces you to learn how to trade profitably and become disciplined.

The trick with trading is to learn from your mistakes, and use them as a guide to create a rules-based trading system which keeps you profitable. Losses will expose the loopholes and weak points in your trading, and it will force you to come up with a plan and system, so that you never face a large loss again.

5. How do you presently trade? (Please give examples along with charts if possible.)

The way that I trade presently is to enter a position just as the stock is breaking out and to always use a stop-loss to mitigate the downside risk. When you mitigate downside risk, you create endless opportunity for the stock to run. You know the most you are willing to lose on the trade is 4–7% at the same time you are creating unlimited upside potential.

The architecture of my trade includes buy point, stop-loss and position size; every trade has a strict criteria and structure. Stock selection is based off fundamentals. I am looking for the strongest stocks from the top sectors and industries in the market. Among these are consecutive increasing sales and EPS during the last 3 quarters, steady increases in fund ownership, high ROI, RS rating above 90, and quality fund ownership. Find the leading industries and sectors in the market, then find the leading stocks from these sectors and industries. Then you dive in and look for quality technical setups in these stocks, this is when the charts come in.

You look for stocks in consolidation phases that are building bases, then watch and wait for these stocks to breakout on high volume. If a stock does not have high volume behind the breakout, which means volume greater than any of the last ten days, then the likelihood of that breakout sticking and working significantly decreases.

The same stock patterns have been repeating themselves since the inception of the stock market; this is where human psychology comes in. As professional investors we understand and recognise these patterns and base our trading around them. Stock charts are a trader's road map and most prized tool. Some of my favourite patterns to trade are bullish pennants, cups with handles, W bottoms and falling wedges.

Below are two of my most profitable trades in 2020. $APPS, Digital Turbine is a company that is listed on the NASDAQ. They develop mobile software that enables mobile content distribution and transactions. From December 2019–June 2020 the company had three consecutive quarters of increasing double-and triple-digit EPS and sales. The company had a 99 RS rating, which means they had stronger relative strength than 99% of the companies in the NASDAQ. This company had some of the strongest fundamentals out there.

I started the position after the stock broke out of the downtrend within the W/double bottom pattern. Then I added onto the position when it broke out of the neckline of the W bottom, making a full-size position. I sold 2 separate quarters into strength and added another half position on the bullish long-legged doji reversal off the 50-day simple moving average (SMA).

I sold one third of my shares into strength then added another half size position when the stock had a triple top breakout. I sold another half into strength then added another half position on the falling wedge breakout. I sold the rest of the shares in small increments while the stock climbed until price broke through the 50-day SMA on heavy volume and could not reclaim it. Once price falls below the key moving averages that price has respected, it is time to exit the trade.

Once price falls below the key moving averages (especially on high volume) which price has respected during the entire run up, and cannot immediately reclaim these moving averages, you should see warning signs flashing. It is the most likely time to immediately exit the trade.

You can see that every breakout where I added onto the position was on high volume. This was

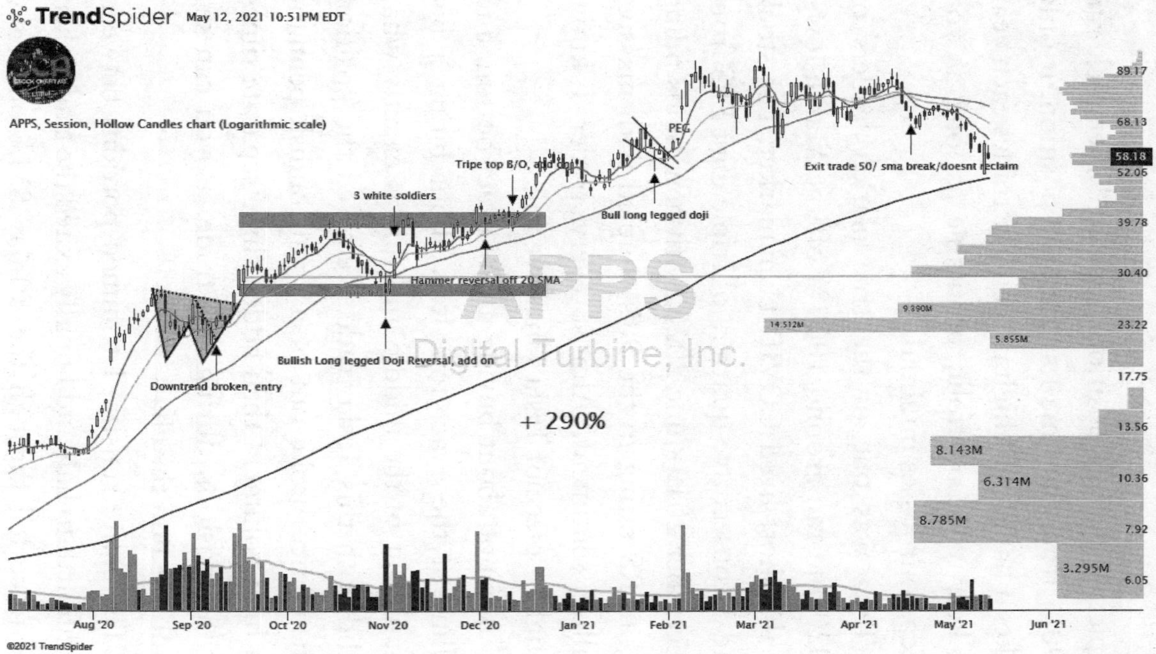

Daily chart of APPS

a picture-perfect position trade and the stock ran 290% from the time I started the position. It only takes a handful of high percentage trades each year to keep your portfolio profitable as long as you keep your losses minimal.

Tesla was one of the true market leaders of 2020 and ran around 1000% off the March lows, of the short-lived COVID bear market. The stock had 3 consecutive quarters of triple digit EPS from December 2019–June 2020, with new funds piling in, an RS rating in the 90's coupled with massive bullish sentiment. Almost every trader I know caught a piece of Tesla's massive run.

It is not about buying at the exact bottom and selling at the exact top. It is about biting a big chunk out of the middle and that is exactly what I did with this Tesla trade. I entered the position when price broke out of a small bullish pennant on high volume. I then added three separate times to this position during this trade, as you can see annotated on the chart.

The entire run up, I trimmed portions between one fourth to half and I finally exited the trade when the price fell through the 50-day SMA on heavy

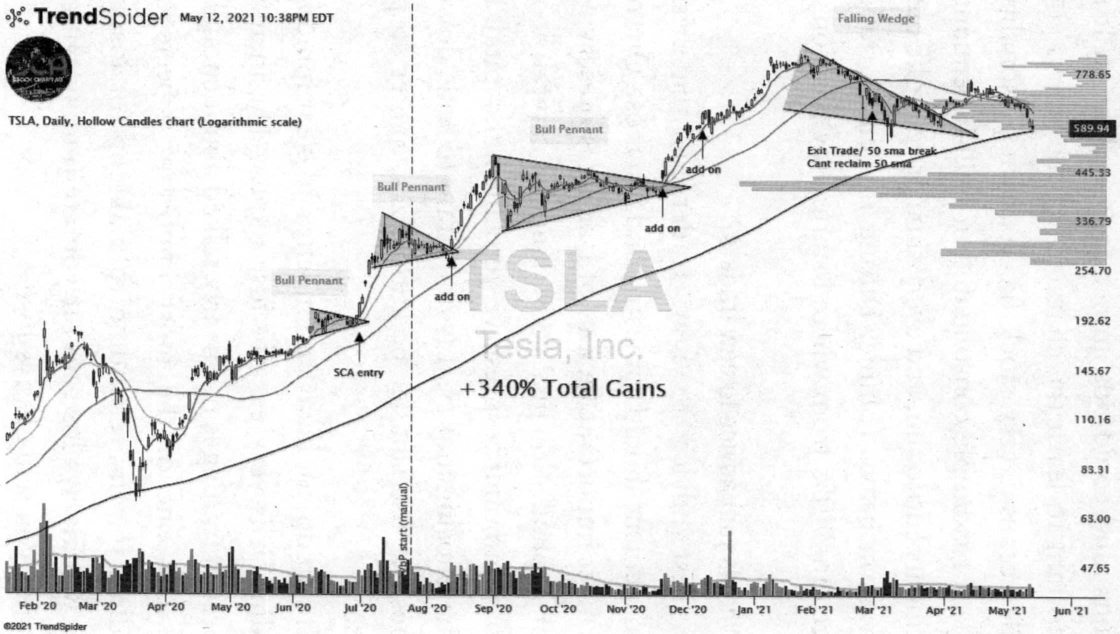

Daily chart for Tesla (TrendSpider)

volume and could not immediately reclaim it. It is important to learn the character of the stocks you trade because every stock has its own personality. Tesla for example consolidated in bullish pennants during its entire run, and every time price broke out, it was on heavy volume. During this entire trade, price ran 340% from where I started my position.

6. What is your advice to new traders?

My best advice to new traders is that risk management should come first and foremost. One of the most important factors of trading is preserving your capital. Not just your financial capital; it is also paramount to preserve your mental capital. If you are losing money, it is important to scale down exposure, use smaller position sizes, tighter stop-losses.

If you do not have a confident and clear mind in trading, it is very easy to lose money. The mental aspect of trading is not nearly talked about enough, yet it is one of the most important aspects of trading. If you are trading to make up for losses, you will always lose, and if you are trading out of revenge you will always lose.

That is why you need to create a clear and simple rules-based system that you can stick to. When the market is not working in your favour it is better to remain all CASH. You do not always have to remain active in the markets, especially during corrections and sideways action which could last months or years. You need to know when to step aside and when to put your foot on the pedal.

Simple rule is if your trades are working, you should gradually increase exposure. If your trades are not working, you should decrease exposure. Always use stop-losses for every single trade, you can always re-enter the trade if it proves itself down the line. Never average down, only average up and add onto a trade when it is working. Use proper position sizing, no more than 10% of your account for one position. If you put 50% of your account into one stock and that stock happens to drop 20% in one day, your entire account is down 10% for the day, which is not encouraging.

Never risk more than 1% of your entire account for each trade. Always lock in profit when it is available; hold on to your core position, but make sure you are always taking profit on the way up.

Keep your losses minimal and let your winners run. Do not worry so much about day to day action once you have a nice cushion in a position; let the stock work for you.

Only consider exiting position if there is a major character change or if price breaks through a key moving average on heavy volume and does not immediately reclaim that moving average. Never impose your will on the market, always let the trades come to you.

7. Which books do you suggest everyone should read?

My three favourite trading books are

- *How to Make Money in Stocks* by William O'Neil
- *Monster Stocks* by John Boik
- *Reminiscences of a Stock Operator* by Jesse Livermore

06

RAJARSHITA SUR

MUMBAI, INDIA

1. Please tell us briefly about your educational background.

My educational background briefly is as follows:

BCom Hons (Calcutta University)

MS Finance (ICFAI)

MBA (ISBM)

2. What were the problems you faced in your initial trading months/years?

Being a novice, I was driven more by emotions and did not practice control over the classic emotions of greed and fear. Only over time was I able to train my mind to control these emotions. Also, I would do a lot of overtrading, jumping from one hope trade to another in search of the Holy Grail. All these led to small losses turning into bigger ones.

Admitting you were wrong and moving on is probably the hardest challenge of them all. It took me more than a year to be able to cut my losses and accept/admit that losses are also part of the trading game.

Once you train your mind and accept this fact, with good risk management practices, you can achieve consistent results. Easier said than done, as sometimes market gyrations can cause continuous losses and you can start to lose confidence, making you feel like an underdog, or a good bull run will cause a mirage in your head that you are the sleekest trader alive; both of which are aberrations.

This is where your mental strength, conviction and good discipline come into play, helping you avoid disastrous losses and assisting you to recuperate quickly, so that you are back in the game. Ultimately, it's all about the nerves!

3. Which markets do you trade and what is your trading style?

Primarily, I focus and trade in Indian equities, earlier global foreign exchange (FX) markets, but also follow commodities closely. I am a swing trader which means I hold positions overnight for several days, hence it is riskier than day trading which could result in large gap up/down openings.

It is imperative that one is able to identify one's personality trait and risk appetite, before choosing the style of trading, which could be a challenging task for newbies. But this is essential for long-term consistency and a peaceful relationship with the markets. If as an anxious person you decide to take positional trades, a large gap up/down could cause your blood vessels to swell with pressure and this is not healthy for your wellbeing or your finances in the long run. Swing trading generally requires a larger stop-loss than day trading, so the ability to keep calm when a trade is against you is a necessity.

4. Did you incur losses when you started trading? How did you overcome that difficult time and stay motivated?

Of course, like every aspiring trader, I too have donated my share of monies to the markets, more during my earlier days and a little every now and then, even today. Losses are like nasty relatives, you may not like them, but you are bound to bump into them occasionally. When you do encounter either (relatives or losses), practise caution and handle with care.

It is paramount that at any cost you ought to protect your capital, as it is with this that you tread the markets and if you extinguish this, your journey culminates. When you take any trade/ position, you start with a 50:50 chance and in spite of where the markets go, it is ultimately your discipline, risk management policies, control over behavioral traits that will help you survive a long and prosperous journey in the markets. The best professional athletes become excited when they discover they have a weakness in their game. They use the weakness as a catalyst to improve.

Some basic principles I adhere to are:

1. *Accept responsibility for your trades/ positions.* It is easy to blame markets, news, events, geopolitical tensions, luck or any other random superstition. However, ultimately you need to have the humility to accept and take ownership. Do as much postmortem as needed but take full responsibility for your actions. Remember,

some news may have caused markets to move against you, but nothing stops you from exiting a position.

2. *Learn from your mistakes or from the postmortem you conduct after a failed trade due to any of umpteen reasons.* The first step towards resolution of a problem is to identify and accept that a shortcoming exists. Ask yourself, where did you fall short? Was the trade well-planned? Were you mentally sharp, or did you hold a losing trade hoping to avoid a loss?

Take a break to figure out what went wrong. Assess what happened by reviewing events carefully. Once identified, inspire yourself to overcome this weakness by constantly persevering in that direction, whether it is deeper study, better skills, or more control over mind and emotions.

5. How do you presently trade? (Please give examples along with charts if possible.)

I follow basic price action for my trading as I like to keep the trading approach simple. A simple approach allows us to clearly see the charts without any biases. Like in the Apollo Hospitals daily chart, you can see how beautifully the stock played out from 1650 to 3400 odd levels.

A trader could have bought it after any of the following breakouts or if someone was already holding this from lower levels, these fresh breakouts provided a chance to add to our winning position.

On the chart for Tata Steel, I have used 50-EMA and was basically waiting for a clean breakout above it along with a trend line breakout. Once the breakout came, the recent swing highs were the next probable targets. Once it gave a breakout, we can keep trailing it with the same 50-EMA.

6. What is your advice to new traders?

- *Before entering financial markets, make sure you have the right tools to help you navigate.* Equip yourself with fundamentals and or technical skills to help analyse price movement before taking a call. Do not put in any money before you have enough knowledge of the markets, the methods of functioning, basic rules and regulations, etc.

Rajarshita_RS published on TradingView.com, May 05, 2021 12:39:20 IST
NSE:APOLLOHOSP, 1D 3205.90 ▲ +24.65 (+0.77%) O:3199.80 H:3239.95 L:3176.15 C:3205.90

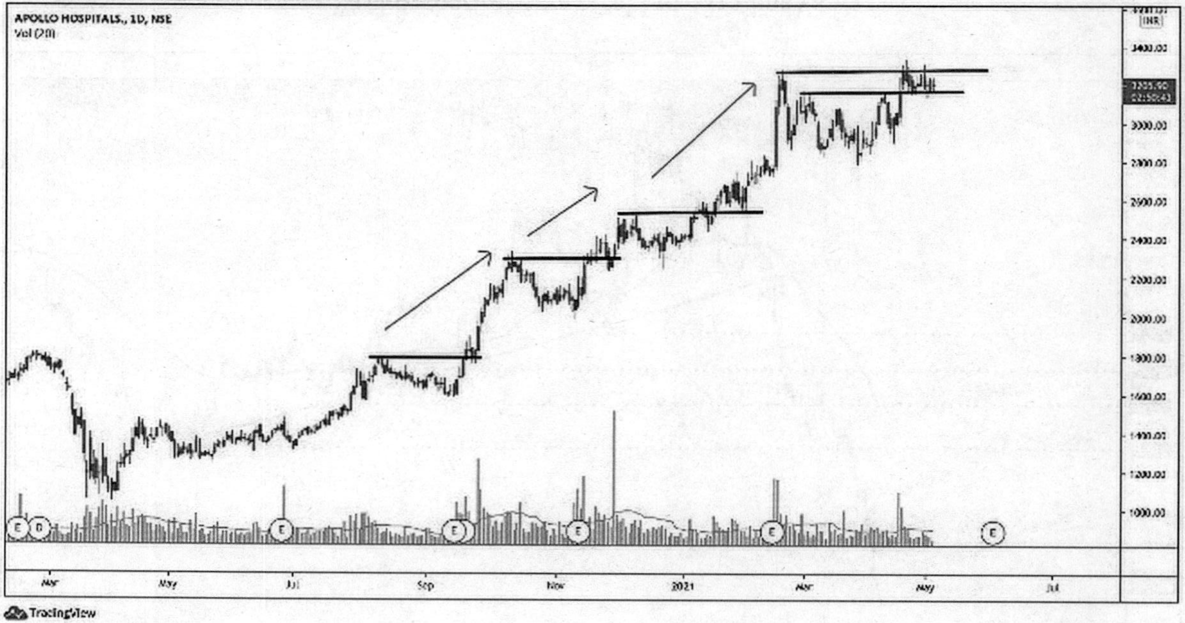

Daily chart of Apollo Hospitals.

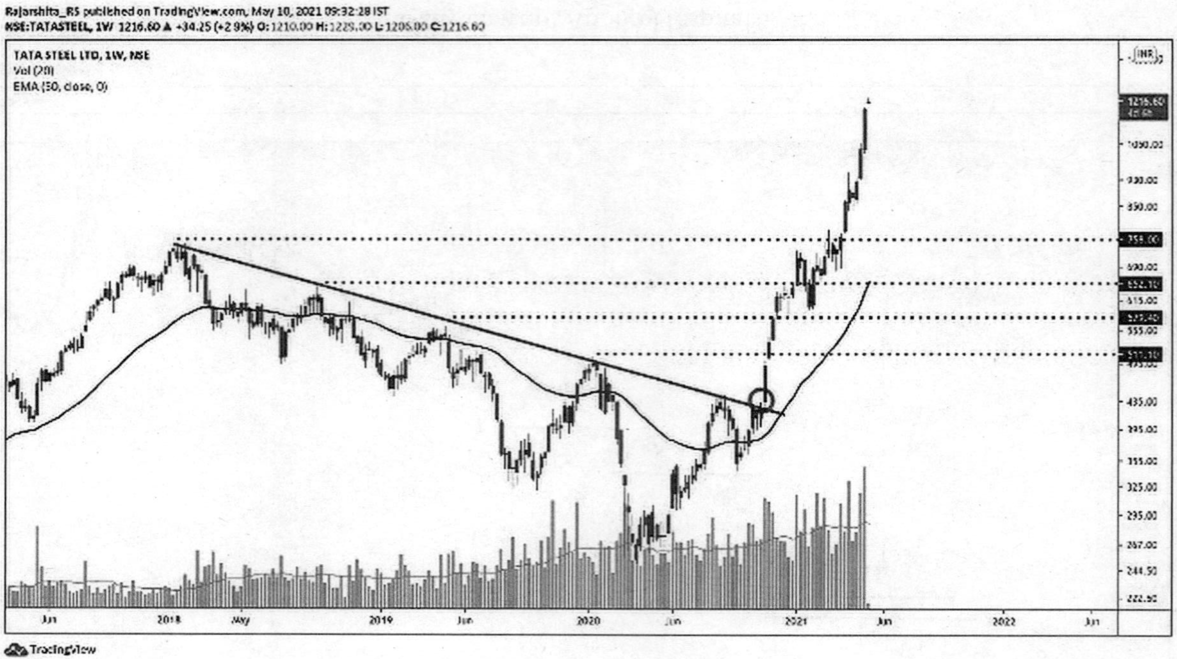

Weekly chart of Tata Steel Ltd. (TradingView)

- *Take enough time to explore markets before you decide to take a plunge.* If you are young, you can try interning with a stock broker, seek help from friends/family who are in the markets, be a dormant but close observer of the happenings and gather enough practical information so as to be able to take basic decisions on your own, before you put your own money to trade.
- *NEVER trade with borrowed capital!* I cannot stress this enough; one should participate in the financial markets ONLY with their own capital, irrespective of how small it is, and do not fall prey to misleading promotions of "doubling" money, "guaranteed" profits and other such rackets. I assure you, with consistency, discipline, and perseverance you can make enough money from the markets *over a period of time* provided you do not treat it like a game of roulette. Also, trade only with authorised dealers and NEVER with any unauthorised/illegal punters like dabba trading.
- *Never start your trading journey with derivatives segment like futures and options as*

a new entrant. Leave this for the professionals or once you have become seasoned over at least a few years (3–4 years), that too if you fully understand ALL the risks and loss potential in ALL scenarios.

- As mentioned earlier, *find a strategy that suits you.* There are plenty of different ways to make money in the market and I believe it is very important to find a strategy that suits your personality, lifestyle, and risk appetite
- Most important is *risk/money management.* Stop-loss is the only Holy Grail in the trading world as nothing else can save you from a disaster. You should have a very clear idea of risk-reward ratio. Say you have INR 100 capital, you should make sure to not lose more than INR 10 on any given trade.

Effectively that leaves you with 10 shots at the market and your given capital and markets have to prove you wrong 10 times consecutively to wipe you out. Probabilistically, there is an odd chance that this will happen if you have a well-thought out strategy and discipline to follow it religiously. Do not feel demotivated if you incur losses at the start, it takes time to become a consistent earning trader, so take your time

- *Take a break!* The human mind is designed to work only a certain number of hours a day after which we max out and require a certain amount of sleep, rest, relaxation. I give utmost importance to my mental health and peace and hence take frequent travel breaks to help me unwind. Remember, the markets are just another source to provide you with money. Nobody enjoys earning money, the real joy is in spending it. For me it is always travelling around the world. Therefore, do take a break and detach from the markets periodically.

7. Which books do you suggest everyone should read?

- *Technical Analysis of the Financial Markets: A Comprehensive Guide to Trading Methods and Applications* by John Murphy
- *A Complete Guide to Volume Price Analysis* by Anna Coulling
- *Market Wizards, Updated: Interviews with Top Traders* by Jack Schwager

- *The Disciplined Trader: Developing Winning Attitudes* by Mark Douglas
- *The Complete Turtle Trader: How 23 Novice Investors Became Overnight Millionaires* by Michael Covel
- *Reminiscence of a Stock Operator* by Jesse Livermore

07

PIYUSH CHAUDHRY

MUMBAI, INDIA

1. Please tell us briefly about your educational background. When did you first hear about the markets?

I am a Bachelors in Commerce, an MBA in Finance and a Cost & Works Accountant. However, I must add that everyone irrespective of their educational backgrounds start in stock markets from scratch.

Though I had heard and read about stock markets throughout my MBA, it was only during one of the sessions on technical analysis that I got interested.

2. What were the problems you faced in your initial trading months/years?

The beginning of my trading career was more like jumping into the pool and learning to swim. In hindsight, and after all these years of being in the market, that was pretty much the worst way of entering the markets.

3. Which markets do you trade and what is your trading style?

The markets we trade depend on our skills and our temperament. My entire focus has always been patterns and the charts in the form of technical analysis per se. Though I started off with classical patterns, it took me several years to get a reasonable grasp of the Elliott Wave Principle. I then learnt coding and coded a few of the strategies that I would generally observe working on the charts. The application of my studies and my temperament suits both cash/futures and that is where I am.

4. Did you incur losses when you started trading? How did you overcome that difficult time and stay motivated?

Well, that is a long list. I think for many years I struggled to make money in the markets. It was as if there was a puzzle somewhere and I was getting better, but in the end would always lose the bet. The illusion that I was getting better along with large overleveraged positions caused me a huge loss in 2008. That year I also lost my job, thanks to attrition.

Much more than a financial shocker, I felt that after all these years of studying, saving and working, if all I could manage was this kind of devastation in my finances, then I must really work on rebuilding myself. Thereon, I set upon a journey of complete change. I have pretty much overhauled myself in all these years. I studied harder and worked on Elliott Wave Principle and trading algorithms, focused on my health and began cutting down all negatives from life. I re-worked on each and every aspect of my life.

5. How do you presently trade? (Please give examples along with charts if possible.)

My trades are primarily into NIFTY, for which I use the wave principle. For the rest, I only take actions as per my automated trading strategies. My long-term investment portfolio is also entirely based on Elliott Wave Principle.

6. What is your advice to new traders?

Trading is about three M's—mind, money and

method. Get all of them right before entering the markets. Start small and build from there.

7. Which books do you suggest everyone should read?

The books that I would recommend are the ones that have helped me immensely.

- *Technical Analsyis of Stock Trends* by Robert Edwards and John Magee
- *Technical Analysis of Financial Markets* by John Murphy
- *Candlesticks Explained* by Gregory Morris
- *Technical Analysis Explained* by Martin Pring
- *Trading for a Living* by Alexander Elder
- *Trading in the Zone* by Mark Douglas
- *Elliott Wave Principle* by Robert Prechter

AUTHOR'S NOTE

Thanks a lot for reading this book. I hope you have gained some important insights about the stock market and the message of the book may pave the path to your successful trading career.

As you may have noticed, all these traders emphasise that mindset is the most important criteria in being a successful trader. This book should help you in achieving that. Good luck and profitable trading!

If you liked this book, I would be really thankful if you post your valuable review on Amazon.

If you wish to follow me on social media for more updates, here are the details:

My Official App:
https://traderharneet.com/
Youtube: Trader Harneet
Instagram: TraderHarneet
Twitter/X: TraderHarneet
Email: Traderharneet@gmail.com